Hold Hope, Wage Peace

Hold Hope, Wage Peace

Inspiring Individuals to Take Action for a Better World

Foreword by Walter Cronkite

Edited by David Krieger and Carah Ong

A Robert Bason Book
Published by Capra Press
155 Canon View Road
Santa Barbara, CA 93108
(805) 969-0203
www.caprapress.com

Cover by Erin Strother, Studio E Graphic Design
Book design by Kathleen Baushke
Body type is Goudy Old Style

Hold hope, wage peace / foreword by Walter Cronkite ; edited by David
Krieger and Carah Ong.
    p. cm.
  "A Robert Bason Book"~T.p. verso.
  ISBN 1-59266-054-1 (trade pbk. : alk. paper) ~ ISBN 1-59266-055-X (limited
signed ed. : alk. paper)
1. Peace. 2. Hope. I. Krieger, David, 1942- II. Ong, Carah, 1979- III.
Title.

  JZ5538.H65 2005
  327.1'72~dc22

  2005015795

  Edition   10   9   8   7   6   5   4   3   2   1

  First Edition

Capra Press
Memorable books since 1969
Santa Barbara

This book is dedicated to
the next generation of peace leaders.

Planethood – The Final Leap to World Peace

*Hope will displace despair and grief when the rule of international law
enforced by international authority replaces the rule of national
force and destruction.*

– Ethel R. Wells

ACKNOWLEDGMENTS

We wish to thank all the authors who contributed chapters to this volume. They share the qualities of dedication, vision and persistence in the pursuit of peace.

Special thanks to eminent journalist Walter Cronkite, the recipient of the Nuclear Age Peace Foundation's 2004 Distinguished Peace Leadership Award, for his kind and wise words in the Foreword.

We thank Howard Zinn for permission to include, "The Optimism of Uncertainty," which was previously published in Loeb, Paul Rogat, *The Impossible Will Take a While: A Citizen's Guide to Hope in a Time of Fear*, New York: Basic Books, 2004. An illustrated version of "100 Ideas for Creating a More Peaceful World" may be found in Chen, Joshua and David Krieger, *Peace 100 Ideas*, San Francisco: CDA Publishers, 2003. "Fifty-One Reasons for Hope" was previously published in Krieger, David, *Today Is Not a Good Day for War*, Santa Barbara: Capra Press, 2005. Appendix B, "Making the United Nations Effective for the 21st Century," was previously published in Ferencz, Benjamin B. and Ken Keyes, Jr., *PlanetHood, The Key to Your Future*, Coos Bay, OR: Love Line Books, 1991.

Our thanks to Bob Bason, publisher of Capra Press, for giving this project his energetic support. Thanks also to Ilene Pritikin and Selma Rubin for proofreading, to Erin Strother and Studio E Graphic Design for the cover design, and to Kathleen Baushke for typesetting.

We also especially thank our friends and colleagues at the Nuclear Age Peace Foundation—board members, advisors, staff and supporters—who are committed to building a world at peace, free of the threat of war and free of weapons of mass destruction. We hope that this book will help to advance the Foundation's mission "to eliminate the nuclear weapons threat to all life, to foster the global rule of law, and to build an enduring legacy of peace through education and advocacy."

CONTENTS

SPECIAL NOTE FOR EDUCATORS AND STUDENTS

If you are an educator or a student, the Nuclear Age Peace Foundation has prepared for your use a special Study Guide for *Hold Hope, Wage Peace*. The Study Guide includes questions for discussion, suggestions for further reading and additional resources to take action. The Study Guide can be downloaded from the Foundation's website at www.wagingpeace.org/hold-hopewagepeace.

"The world is a dangerous place to live; not because of the people who are evil, but because of the people who don't do anything about it."

– Albert Einstein

"If you are neutral in situations of injustice, you have chosen the side of the oppressor."

– Archbishop Desmond Tutu

"There is nothing more powerful than an individual acting out of conscience, thus bringing the collective conscience to life."

– Norman Cousins

FOREWORD
Walter Cronkite

It was called at first simply "the atomic bomb." The United States invented and built it and used it to destroy two large Japanese cities and kill tens of thousands of their citizens. Japan sued for peace, ending World War II.

Within a few years the Russians announced the end of America's nuclear monopoly. The Soviets had developed their own bomb and there rose the real possibility that a nuclear war and the resultant poisoning of the globe's atmosphere would seriously threaten all life on this planet—human, flora and fauna.

Despite the magnitude of that threat, efforts to achieve mutual nuclear disarmament led down blind alleys. Instead the best that the best brains in Washington and Moscow could conceive was the promise that one nation's use of the bomb would prompt instant retaliation by the other.

This policy of unimaginable horror was called Mutual Assured Destruction, or "MAD" for short. It seemed to work, at least to the desired extent that the two original nuclear powers did not unleash their insane weapons. The problem is that others of the major nations soon developed their own nuclear armaments. And now, thanks in part to the perfidy and greed of Pakistan's top nuclear scientist who peddled weapon-building know-how worldwide, we don't know how many small nations and would-be terrorists are seeking or are in possession of atomic bombs or, at the very least, the materials or the knowledge of how to make them.

This frightening reality burdens us all with a sense of hopelessness over civilization's future. But hopelessness translates into inaction; it translates into surrender to what is feared to be the inevitable.

We must all be thinking about what can be done to assure a human future on our planet. As the survivors of Hiroshima and Nagasaki, the *hibakusha*, have continually warned, "Nuclear weapons and human beings cannot co-exist."

As a species we are neither smart enough nor careful enough to continue to live with nuclear weapons in our midst. So far we have been lucky that since the end of World War II nuclear weapons have not been used again in war. But there is no telling how long this luck will hold, and we cannot count on it indefinitely.

David Krieger and the Nuclear Age Peace Foundation are determined that there shall be no such surrender, that hopelessness will be replaced by hope among the world's people. That is the theme of this book of remarkable essays by some of our great thinkers that he has assembled to bolster the legitimacy and the necessity of hope and peace.

One of Krieger's own contributions to this volume is the credo of his faith in hope. It is a faith that has guided him for more than two decades. That is how long ago he and others founded the Nuclear Age Peace Foundation and established and nurtured its efforts around the world for peace and an end to the nuclear weapons threat to all life. He has received recognition and awards for his efforts, and success, in educating the people and keeping before the world's governments their plea for nuclear disarmament.

He has inspired many people including this writer. I carried something of his philosophy and determination to a baccalaureate speech to the 2004 graduating class of California's distinguished Pomona College.

I noted the billions of dollars our Defense Department spends to develop new means to kill more thousands of people with greater efficiency and the lack of any nearly similar expenditure to preserve world peace.

I dared suggest that we might convince our own people and the world of our determination to achieve lasting world peace by concentrating our effort in a full staffed and well-funded Department of Peace.

To give it a running start, I even suggested the Department of State could well become the Department of Peace with transfer to it of much of its skilled personnel, prestige and international recognition. Our embassies abroad and our consulates would fly alongside the Stars and Stripes the flag of the Department of Peace to remind all of this nation's determination to give to peace the full attention we now give to war.

The new Department would have its educational facilities to rival West Point, Annapolis, the U.S. Air Force Academy and Marine Corps University. It would train generations of scholars, planners, intelligence forces and diplomats whose learned skills would be concentrated on the preservation of peace.

I like to think that David Krieger and the Nuclear Age Peace Foundation would endorse this as a means of certifying our quest for world peace and thus justify our hope for the future of our globe.

THE POWER OF ONE
David Krieger

This book will be a success if it inspires you to be a force for creating a better world. Nothing great has ever happened without individual initiative and each of us has the potential to make significant contributions. George Kennan, a distinguished American diplomat, said, "If humanity is to have a hopeful future, there is no escape from the pre-eminent involvement and responsibility of the single human soul, in all its loneliness and frailty." He's right. Great achievements begin with individual initiative and are successful because individuals persevere, at times overcoming seemingly insuperable obstacles, in seeing their goals through to completion. The best thing about the *power of one* is that it resides in each of us.

We humans are uniquely equipped with minds capable of thought, hearts capable of compassion, and consciences capable of discerning right from wrong. We have voices that can speak out and feet that can take a stand. These are truly wonderful capacities; they are ours to use if we choose.

With so many serious problems in the world, such as starvation, disease and war, we cannot just sit back and wait for others find solutions. First, it won't just happen, and second, it diminishes us not to engage in the important issues of our time. The truth is that the world needs each of us. Part of our journey here must be to contribute to building a better world. The future will be shaped by each of us: by our insights or our ignorance; by our actions or our apathy; by our contributions or our complacency. We are each challenged to find a way to contribute our own particular talents to the great causes of peace, justice, human dignity and the survival of life on our planet.

In our actions, we can be guided by our compassion and empathy for others, and also by the examples of extraordinary individuals who have accomplished remarkable achievements for humanity. One thinks of Mahatma Gandhi nonviolently defeating British imperialism; of Martin Luther King, Jr. non-violently leading the civil rights movement in the United States and then moving on to give leadership to the struggles against poverty and the war in Vietnam; of Mother Teresa giving aid and comfort to the poor and infirm in the slums of Calcutta; and of Nelson Mandela coming out after 27 years of impris-onment to become president of his country, end apartheid in South Africa, and use the power of forgiveness to help heal the deep wounds left by decades of racial injustice. These are just some of the individuals whose lives can inspire us to higher levels of commitment and action to build a better world.

Of course, we cannot all be leaders like these, but each of us in our own way can work for peace, justice, human dignity and, above all, the continuation of life on our planet. To do so, we must begin with an awareness of the serious problems of war, injustice, human rights abuses and threats to our com-mon future. We cannot allow ourselves to drift in ignorance and apathy as tens of millions of our fellow humans around the world suffer and die and even greater disasters loom ahead. We are challenged to extend our compassion beyond the artificial constructs of national boundaries to every corner of the globe.

The emphasis in this book is on hope and peace. The two are intimately interrelated. Hope is an impetus to action, and action reinforces hope. Hope is far more than just optimism. It isn't just thinking that the world *may* become better in some magical way; rather, it is the conviction that one's efforts can help create change for the better. The opposite of hope is despair, a condition that limits action. Despair gives birth to apathy and ignorance. Despair leads to withdrawal, while hope leads to engagement. Hope is a far better foundation for accepting the challenges that life offers us. It is positive and action-oriented. It is a starting point for accepting individual responsibility for making a difference in the world.

Peace, in all its dimensions, has become an imperative of our time. In the Nuclear Age we can no longer afford to run the risk of resolving conflicts by means of war. It is simply too dangerous to do so. Nuclear arsenals could destroy our great cities, our civilizations and even bring an end to most life on earth. In 1955, Albert Einstein and Bertrand Russell, two of the great intellectual leaders of the 20th century, issued a manifesto in which they warned of nuclear dangers to humanity. They wrote: "Here, then, is the problem which we present to you, stark and dreadful and inescapable: Shall we put an end to the human race; or shall mankind renounce war?" Fifty years later, this warning is still valid; we ignore it at our peril.

Perhaps you are thinking, "Well, all of this sounds fine, but I am only one person, and what can I really do to change the world?" It is a good question, but one that can't be answered for you. Ultimately, each of us must answer this question for oneself. One thing is clear: we each have all the human qualities that are needed to make a difference in creating a better world. But we must each begin with a first step. Perhaps you have already taken that step, or perhaps you are ready to do so now.

Changing the world can begin with increasing your awareness and paying more attention to what is happening in the world. This book is meant to help you on the path to increasing your awareness and understanding of serious global problems, and hopefully to help you think about these problems in a new way—a way that demands your involvement.

It can begin as simply as making up your mind to make a difference. We all have the *power of one* within us, and each of us can become as powerful a force for change as we choose to be. Our initiatives and perseverance can help shape a more peaceful and decent world.

The potential world of the future, waiting to be born—a world of peace, justice and human dignity—is in our hands and hearts. We must treat this potential world, as well as the one we live in, with respect. The world of the future is ours to create and to pass on to future generations.

There is a Zen saying that one chops wood and carries water before enlightenment; and after enlightenment one chops wood and carries water. In other words, the basics don't change with enlightenment. Our thesis is that the basics for building a more decent world are holding hope and waging peace, and that these do not change.

Our hope at the Nuclear Age Peace Foundation is that this book can help you to find and develop the power within yourself to contribute to building a world in which all people can live with dignity. The world needs each of us to stand up, speak out and be a force for peace. We each must do our part in holding hope and waging peace.

Hold
Hope

"Everything that is done in the world is done by hope."

— Martin Luther King, Jr.

"Hope is not the conviction that something will turn out well, but the certainty that something makes sense regardless of how it turns out."

— Vaclav Havel

"The capacity for hope is the most significant fact of life. It provides human beings with a sense of destination and the energy to get started."

— Norman Cousins

HOPE FOR PEACE
Jane Goodall

Mahatma Gandhi said that if you looked back through history you would find that every evil, ultimately, was overcome by good. Whilst this is a comforting thought, could we not equally say that evil ultimately overcomes good? In other words, after a period of peace is war inevitable? If we accept the concept of evolution and believe (as I do) that we, along with the modern great apes, have evolved during the millennia from an ape-like, human-like ancestor, then it does seem that we have probably inherited aggressive tendencies from our ancient primate past. Chimpanzees, biologically closer to us than are the other great apes—the structure of their DNA differs from ours by only about one percent—have a dark side to their nature and are capable of acts of brutality and even a kind of primitive warfare. Does this mean that we cannot escape our legacy of violence, that war is inevitable? I passionately disagree. For one thing, the explosive development of the human intellect has equipped us with a tool capable of (in the absence of clinical psychiatric problems) controlling any aggressive "instincts" we may have. Which most people do, most of the time. For another, chimpanzees also show highly developed traits of compassion, love and altruism. We must choose which path to take.

It is true that wars have dogged humanity's progress throughout recorded history, yet there are places that seem to have left their bloody past behind. As one travels in Britain, France,

Germany, Holland, Italy and Spain today, it is hard to imagine the bitter fighting that once raged, the horrific conditions in which soldiers fought—on foot, on horseback, in the trenches, with bows and arrows, long bows, lances, bayonets, and cannons. There were terrible civil wars in England and Spain—horrible wars dividing families and friends and inciting them to kill their own. The whole of Europe was embroiled in the horrors of the two World Wars. Yes, the past history of Europe was violent, cruel and bloody. Yet now more and more countries are joining the European Union and living in harmony with each other.

For America it is the same. There was a time when there was bitter fighting between different states. There was the civil war between North and South, fought in principle to end slavery in America, when over 650,000 Americans were killed by Americans, more than the combined total of those who died in all other American wars. And there was cruel genocide as the white invaders, along with their diseases, killed Native Americans by the thousands, and drove them from their tribal lands. Yet now the States are united under the star-spangled banner, one star for each state, and all living in peace. Even the Native Americans, while still suffering major injustices, are at least free to practice their ancient ceremonies, perpetuate their languages, and many of them now feel pride in who they are.

Desperation and Terrorism

And so perhaps we can dare to hope that for some of the warring factions around the world today, a similar peaceful future lies ahead—sometime within the present century. But what about terrorism? Groups of desperate people, driven to fight for their cause against military power that they could never defeat during normal armed conflict, striking out unexpectedly, often against the innocent. Their methods are many: kidnapping, suicide bombing, car bombs, hostage-taking, destroying property and life—even piloting planes into buildings. Terrorists may be religious fanatics fueled by feelings of righteousness. Or they may be fighting, in the only way they know how, to free their people from oppression. But even if their cause seems worthy, their methods, when they strike out against innocent people, are despicable—and do indeed inspire terror.

Terrorism is by no means a new phenomenon, although the events of 9/11 brought it forcefully to the attention of Americans. *But it has proliferated around the world. Is it possible that some of this hatred may be fueled by a sense of unbearable injustice?* As we all know, the gap between the rich and the poor is ever widening. This is, at least partly, due to the dark side of corporate globalization that bribes poor countries—with promises of future wealth and improved living conditions—to part with their precious, ever-dwindling natural resources. The imposition of modern agriculture methods diverts land from its traditional use, and too often the bulk of revenue from the export of commodities goes straight into corrupt pockets. Many nonrenewable resources are squandered as developing countries struggle to pay off huge debts. Meanwhile, as the elite maintain their unsustainable materialistic life styles, the poor for the most part get poorer. So long as people are hopeless, oppressed by poverty, hunger, disease and ignorance, there will be those willing to take up arms to fight for their rights, even to give up their lives—out of sheer frustration and desperation. They have so little to lose.

Nonviolent Tactics

Yet while victories have indeed been won through armed conflict, non-violent tactics have also brought success. There is a glittering array of heroic figures who have realized the power of peaceful protest to effect change. Jesus himself argued for turning the other cheek. Mahatma Gandhi used principles of nonviolence to free India from colonial rule. Martin Luther King upheld nonviolent methods in his successful struggle to abolish the segregation laws in the Deep South. Nelson Mandela developed the power to forgive his enemies during his 23 years in prison, and so led his country from the evil regime of apartheid without a blood bath. The Berlin Wall eventually came down without fighting. In 2000, Slobodan Milosevic was defeated by an ingenious nonviolent strategy of honest elections and widespread civil disobedience. It was a student-led organization, comprised of human rights and pro-democracy activists that inspired the people to vote the "Butcher of the Balkans" out of office. When he refused to accept defeat, Serbians by the hundreds of thousands descended on the capital and seized the parliament in a dramatic triumph for non-violence and democracy.

Of course, nonviolence does not always work. The haunting photo of the student, standing alone to confront the power of government forces in Tiananmen Square in Beijing, will always remind us that peaceful demonstration can fail. Yet the actions of the students and their supporters—and the very fact that this took place at all—will remain a landmark in the history of modern China. So also will the unprecedented demonstrations that took place during the months preceding the March 19, 2003 attack on Iraq, in which more citizens from around the globe than ever before in human history came out onto the streets to protest war and to make their voices heard. But all the demonstrations, protests and prayers were disregarded. And so the enthusiasm and optimism of all the millions who raised their voices against war was squelched. Many, succumbing to understandable feelings of hopelessness and depression, have become apathetic. Some have become furiously angry. In America, this anger against the administration, coupled with feelings of powerlessness to do anything about it, is causing many people to think of emigrating, getting away from it all.

But those seeking peace must never give up. Instead we must work even harder. For if all of the millions—nay, billions—of citizens around the world who truly care about the state of our planet, about the future of their children and their children's children, fall into apathy and carry on with business as usual, or run away and hide, we shall be judged poorly by generations to come. Achieving peace will not be easy, for discontent and resentment will continue to grow, and the natural world with all its rich and wondrous creatures will increasingly be destroyed, until we address the unequal distribution of wealth around the globe. And until we learn to live in greater harmony with nature there can be no lasting peace. So it is desperately important that each one of us plays our part. Yet we feel so helpless. One among more than 6 billion: *what difference*, you think, *can I make?* But you are not alone. There are billions who feel like you. And individual actions that benefit the environment or society, when multiplied millions of times over, create huge change. We can all be linked through the internet, giving each other support and courage. Moreover, all the time our numbers are swelling. Let each one of us, therefore, vow never to give up.

Reasons for Hope

I am always asked if, in this very dangerous world today, I honestly have hope for the future. And I always answer "Yes—but only if we all roll up our sleeves and get into the action." My four main reasons for hope—for the environment and our human future—are these: (1) We are a problem-solving species that has evolved an extraordinarily sophisticated brain and—just in time I think—we have woken to the real harm we have perpetrated on the natural world, and on human society. We have started to link brains *and hearts* around the world and have begun to come up with ingenious solutions to many of our problems; (2) Mother Nature is amazingly resilient if we give her a chance and a helping hand. Land that has been destroyed can be restored and animals on the brink of extinction can be given another chance; (3) There is what I refer to as the indomitable human spirit—so many people tackle seemingly impossible tasks, and succeed. People in all walks of life inspire those around them with their determination, their courage, and their faith in humanity; and finally, (4) Young people, once they understand the nature of the problems, and are empowered to act, show such energy and enthusiasm and creativity that they truly effect change.

It was when I realized, eleven years ago, that so many young people around the world were without hope—apathetic, depressed or bitter—that I knew I had to try to help. They felt we had compromised their future—and we have. I know true anguish when I look at my grandchildren and think how we have harmed the world since I was their age. And this has led to my deep involvement with youth, particularly with our Roots & Shoots program. It is a symbolic name: Roots make a firm foundation and Shoots seem small, but together they can break open brick walls. Imagine the walls as all of the problems we have inflicted on the planet and here is the message of hope— hundreds and thousands of young people can break through and make a better world. We help students to understand what is going on, and the major role they can play, as individuals, in putting things right. They are empowered to take informed and compassionate action on behalf of animals, human beings and the environment. Our Peace Initiative encourages them to learn more about those whose language, religion, ethnic group and country are different from theirs. We help them to understand that there is a huge difference between moderate Muslims, Christians and Jews, and the fanatics that seem to emerge in all religions. Some groups study conflict resolution, working out different solutions to a variety of problems. Then they act out one scenario based on aggression and violence, and one on negotiation, respect and understanding. Our policy is to form partnerships, to collaborate with those of like mind, and we have become aware of many other organizations for young people with similar goals. We are trying to create a critical mass of youth to help us wage peace, for they will be taking over businesses, scientific research, and governance in the future.

Kofi Annan asked me to become one of his Messengers of Peace following a discussion we had during our first meeting about Roots & Shoots. I told him about our nonviolent philosophy: changing attitudes not through guns, bombs, or any other kind of violence, but through knowledge and understanding, hard work and persistence, and love and compassion leading to respect for all life. I told him that we were trying to break down the artificial barriers that have been built between people of different countries, different religions, different ethnic groups, different cultures, and also between people and animals. Today there are over 7,500 active *groups* in more than 80 countries, with an age range from pre-school through university. We are truly, I told him, sowing seeds for global peace.

THE OPTIMISM OF UNCERTAINTY
Howard Zinn

In this awful world where the efforts of caring people often pale in comparison to what is done by those who have power, how do I manage to stay involved and seemingly happy?

I am totally confident not that the world will get better, but that we should not give up the game before all the cards have been played. The metaphor is deliberate; life is a gamble. Not to play is to foreclose any chance of winning. To play, to act, is to create at least a possibility of changing the world.

There is a tendency to think that what we see in the present moment will continue. We forget how often we have been astonished by the sudden crumbling of institutions, by extraordinary changes in people's thoughts, by unexpected eruptions of rebellion against tyrannies, by the quick collapse of systems of power that seemed invincible.

The Unpredictability of History

What leaps out from the history of the past hundred years is its utter unpredictability. A revolution to overthrow the czar of Russia, in that most sluggish of semi-feudal empires, not only startled the most advanced imperial powers but took Lenin himself by surprise and sent him rushing by train to Petrograd. Who would have predicted the bizarre shifts of World War II--the Nazi-Soviet pact (those embarrassing photos of von

Ribbentrop and Molotov shaking hands), and the German Army rolling through Russia, apparently invincible, causing colossal casualties, being turned back at the gates of Leningrad, on the western edge of Moscow, in the streets of Stalingrad, followed by the defeat of the German army, with Hitler huddled in his Berlin bunker, waiting to die?

And then the postwar world, taking a shape no one could have drawn in advance: The Chinese Communist revolution, the tumultuous and violent Cultural Revolution, and then another turnabout, with post-Mao China renouncing its most fervently held ideas and institutions, making overtures to the West, cuddling up to capitalist enterprise, perplexing everyone.

No one foresaw the disintegration of the old Western empires happening so quickly after the war, or the odd array of societies that would be created in the newly independent nations, from the benign village socialism of Nyerere's Tanzania to the madness of Idi Amin's adjacent Uganda. Spain became an astonishment. I recall a veteran of the Abraham Lincoln Brigade telling me that he could not imagine Spanish Fascism being overthrown without another bloody war. But after Franco was gone, a parliamentary democracy came into being, open to Socialists, Communists, anarchists, everyone.

The end of World War II left two superpowers with their respective spheres of influence and control, vying for military and political power. Yet they were unable to control events, even in those parts of the world considered to be their respective spheres of influence. The failure of the Soviet Union to have its way in Afghanistan, and its decision to withdraw after almost a decade of ugly intervention, was the most striking evidence that even the possession of thermonuclear weapons does not guarantee domination over a determined population. The United States has faced the same reality. It waged a full-

scale war in Indochina, conducting the most brutal bombard-
ment of a tiny peninsula in world history, and yet was forced
to withdraw. In the headlines every day we see other instances
of the failure of the presumably powerful over the presumably
powerless, as in Brazil, where a grassroots movement of workers
and the poor elected a new president pledged to fight destructive corporate power.

Looking at this catalogue of huge surprises, it's clear that
the struggle for justice should never be abandoned because of
the apparent overwhelming power of those who have the guns
and the money and who seem invincible in their determination
to hold on to it. That apparent power has, again and again,
proved vulnerable to human qualities less measurable than
bombs and dollars: moral fervor, determination, unity, organization, sacrifice, wit, ingenuity, courage, patience—whether by
blacks in Alabama and South Africa; peasants in El Salvador,
Nicaragua and Vietnam; or workers and intellectuals in Poland,
Hungary and the Soviet Union itself. No cold calculation of
the balance of power need deter people who are persuaded
that their cause is just.

I have tried hard to match my friends in their pessimism
about the world (is it just my friends?), but I keep encounter-
ing people who, in spite of all the evidence of terrible things
happening everywhere, give me hope. Especially young people,
in whom the future rests. Wherever I go, I find such people.
And beyond the handful of activists there seem to be hundreds,
thousands more, who are open to unorthodox ideas. But they
tend not to know of one another's existence, and so, while
they persist, they do so with the desperate patience of Sisyphus
endlessly pushing that boulder up the mountain. I try to tell
each group that it is not alone, and that the very people who
are disheartened by the absence of a national movement are
themselves proof of the potential for such a movement.

Small Acts Can Transform the World

Revolutionary change does not come as one cataclysmic moment (beware of such moments!) but as an endless succession of surprises, moving zigzag toward a more decent society. We don't have to engage in grand, heroic actions to participate in the process of change. Small acts, when multiplied by millions of people, can transform the world. Even when we don't "win," there is fun and fulfillment in the fact that we have been involved, with other good people, in something worthwhile. We need hope.

An optimist isn't necessarily a blithe, slightly sappy, whistler-in-the-dark of our time. To be hopeful in bad times is not just foolishly romantic. It is based on the fact that human history is a history not only of cruelty but also of compassion, sacrifice, courage, kindness.

What we choose to emphasize in this complex history will determine our lives. If we see only the worst, it destroys our capacity to do something. If we remember those times and places--and there are so many--where people have behaved magnificently, this gives us the energy to act, and at least the possibility of sending this spinning top of a world in a different direction. And if we do act, in however small a way, we don't have to wait for some grand utopian future. The future is an infinite succession of presents, and to live now as we think human beings should live, in defiance of all that is bad around us, is itself a marvelous victory.

MAKING HOPE
Daisaku Ikeda

Looking at the world today, it is easy to feel despair. The hopeful mood with which we greeted the new century seems to have faded, replaced by widespread feelings of frustration and hopelessness. A kind of powerlessness seems to be the prevailing mood in the world today. Decisions about important issues all seem to be made somewhere beyond our reach. What can one person accomplish in the face of the vast forces that run our world? The current of the times can seem so fast-flowing and complex as to be overwhelming.

Everything Begins with Us

I do not believe that people are powerless. The philosophical tradition which I embrace in fact takes exactly the opposite view. Buddhism focuses on the most fundamental dimension—that of life itself—teaching that each human life partakes of the limitless life force of the cosmos. The same power which moves the universe exists within our lives. Each individual has immense potential—and a great change in the inner dimension of one individual's life has the power to touch the lives of others and transform society. Everything begins with us.

As Nigerian author and poet Ben Okri has written:

> You can't remake the world
> Without remaking yourself.
> Each new era begins within.
> It is an inward event,
> With unsuspected possibilities
> For inner liberation.

The term my mentor, Josei Toda, used for this process of inner transformation that also transforms our surroundings was "human revolution." And I believe it is the most fundamental and most vital of all revolutions. It can create changes that are more lasting and valuable than political, economic or technological revolutions. For no matter how external factors change, the world will never get better as long as people remain selfish and apathetic.

An inner change for the better in a single person—one person becoming wiser, stronger, more compassionate—is the essential first turn of the wheel toward realizing peaceful coexistence and fulfillment for the whole human race. I firmly believe that a great human revolution in just one person can be the start of a transformation in the destiny of whole societies and all humankind. And for the individual, everything starts in the inner reaches of life itself.

When we change our inner determination, everything begins to move in a new direction. The moment we make a powerful resolve, every nerve and fiber in our being will immediately orient itself toward the fulfillment of that goal or desire. On the other hand, if we think, "This is never going to work out," then every cell in our body will be deflated and give up the fight.

Hope Is a Decision

Hope, in this sense, is a decision. It is the most important decision we can make. Hope changes everything, starting with our lives. Hope is the force that enables us to take action to make our dreams come true. It has the power to change winter to summer, barrenness to creativity, agony to joy. As long as we have hope, there is nothing we cannot achieve. When we possess the treasure of hope, we can draw forth our inner potential and strength. A person of hope can always advance.

Hope is a flame that we nurture within our hearts. It may be sparked by someone else—by the encouraging words of a friend, relative or mentor—but it must be fanned and kept burning through our own determination. Most crucial is our determination to continue to believe in the limitless dignity and possibilities of both ourselves and others.

Mahatma Gandhi led the nonviolent struggle for Indian independence from British colonial rule, succeeding against all odds. He was, in his own words, "an irrepressible optimist." His hope was not based on circumstances, rising and falling as things seemed to be going better or worse. Rather, it was based on an unshakable faith in humanity, in the capacity of people for good. He absolutely refused to abandon his faith in his fellow human beings.

Keeping faith in people's essential goodness, and the consistent effort to cultivate this goodness in ourselves—as Gandhi proved, these are the twin keys to unleashing the great power of hope. Believing in ourselves and in others in this way—continuing to wage the difficult inner struggle to make this the basis for our actions—can transform a society that sometimes seems to be plummeting toward darkness into a humane and enlightened world where all people are treated with respect.

There may be times when, confronted by cruel reality, we verge on losing all hope. If we cannot feel hope, it is time to create some. We can do this by digging deeper within, searching for even a small glimmer of light, for the possibility of a way to begin to break through the impasse before us. And our capacity for hope can actually be expanded and strengthened by difficult circumstances. Hope that has not been tested is nothing more than a fragile dream. Hope begins from this challenge, this effort to strive towards an ideal, however distant it may seem.

The Tragedy of Losing Hope

It is far better to pursue a remote, even seemingly impossible goal than to cheat ourselves of the forward motion that such goals can provide. I believe that the ultimate tragedy in life is not physical death. Rather, it is the spiritual death of losing hope, giving up on our own possibilities for growth.

My mentor, Josei Toda, once wrote: "In looking at great people of the past, we find that they remained undefeated by life's hardships, by life's pounding waves. They held fast to hopes that seemed mere fantastic dreams to other people. They let nothing stop or discourage them from realizing their aspirations. The reason for this, I feel certain, is that their hopes themselves were not directed toward the fulfillment of personal desires or self-interest, but based on a wish for all people's happiness, and this filled them with extraordinary conviction and confidence."

Here he pointed to a crucially important truth: real hope is found in committing ourselves to vast goals and dreams—dreams such as a world without war and violence, a world where everyone can live in dignity.

The problems that face our world are daunting in their depth and complexity. Sometimes it may be hard to see where—or how—to begin. But we cannot be paralyzed by despair. We must each take action toward the goals we have set and in which we believe. Rather than passively accepting things as they are, we must embark on the challenge of creating a new reality. It is in that effort that true, undying hope is to be found.

THE GROWING POWER OF THE WORLD'S PEOPLE: A REASON FOR HOPE

Douglas Roche

In many ways, the prospects for peace and disarmament were far greater at the 10th anniversary of the Nuclear Age Peace Foundation in 1992 than they are today. At that time the post-Cold War era was still young, and there was lingering hope that the world's people would realize a "peace dividend" as governments diverted military spending to projects fostering human development, both at home and abroad. The awesome destructive power of nuclear weapons, justified for so long by Western and Communist bloc powers as required for deterrence, seemed likely to be discarded along with the antagonistic quality that used to characterize relations between the superpowers.

By 2004, however, it is clear that governments have ignored the opportunity to redirect resources to peacebuilding and development initiatives, preferring instead to expand their own military power. World military spending has grown by leaps and bounds in response to the terrorist attacks of September 11, 2001, while development spending has not seen commensurate increases, and still languishes far below the United Nations target of 0.7 percent GDP in all but a few developed states.

The Nuclear Weapons States (NWS) of China, France, Russia, the United Kingdom and the United States have abused the terms of the Nuclear Non-Proliferation Treaty (NPT), which allowed them to retain their nuclear weapons on condition that they enter into negotiations directed at complete nuclear disarmament. Instead, some of the NWS have been eager to enforce the terms of the NPT on Non-Nuclear Weapons States such as Iran and North Korea, while refusing to meet their own obligation to disarm. China, along with the U.S., has yet to ratify the Comprehensive Test Ban Treaty, and is refusing to participate in any nuclear disarmament measures until the U.S. and Russia have drastically reduced their own arsenals. For its part, Russia has forsaken its policy of never being the first to use nuclear weapons, and under its new Strategic Concept released in 2000, is reserving the right to use nuclear weapons when under attack, even if its adversary does not have a nuclear capacity.

Not content with its vastly superior conventional forces, the United States is refusing to reduce its nuclear arsenal and has recently opted to create new roles for its nuclear weapons. The Moscow Treaty, the most recent arms "reduction" treaty between Russia and the U.S., will only limit the number of nuclear weapons deployed, and will not require the destruction of a single warhead. Despite making, along with the other NWS during the 2000 Review of the NPT, an "unequivocal undertaking" to negotiate nuclear disarmament, the U.S. is pressing ahead with research on new so-called "low yield" nuclear weapons which it plans on incorporating into warfighting doctrine and practice. Having rejected its own NPT obligations, the U.S. still intends to enforce the NPT's provisions on other states through programs such as the Proliferation Security Initiative, aimed at intercepting weapons of mass destruction in transit between states on the high seas. To protect itself against the predictable backlash from states such as North Korea, which insist on keeping the nuclear weapons option open in the absence of an enforceable security guarantee, the U.S. has embarked on an ambitious program of Ballistic Missile Defense, which has shown little promise of surmounting significant technical obstacles and affording real protection to the American homeland.

Make no mistake: the NPT, which promised to forestall nuclear weapons programs in non-nuclear weapons states until the nuclear powers could negotiate disarmament, is in crisis. The acknowledged nuclear capability of India and Pakistan and the virtual certainty of an Israeli nuclear capacity are augmented by North Korean threats to consummate its nuclear program with a weapons test, and the disturbing possibility that the regime could sell its nuclear technology and materials to others. While American threats and promises may succeed in temporarily capping this particular program, it is difficult to imagine that U.S. adversaries will agree indefinitely to forgo nuclear programs in light of the overwhelming dominance of American military power and the threat it poses to their security. In short, the complete elimination of the world's nuclear weapons, which the Final Document of the 2000 NPT Review called "the only absolute guarantee" against nuclear war, seems farther off than ever.

The Growing Power of the World's People

However, if the actions and policies of the world's governments provide reasons for despair, the growing power of the world's people is a reason for hope. People are waking up to the fact that they share common interests and a common fate, and that these interests are not always accurately reflected by their governments. As a result, people from a wide diversity of religious, ethnic and national backgrounds are working together to advance the causes of peace and development through civil society groups and NGOs.

Among these organizations are groups such as Amnesty International, the Canadian Centre for International Cooperation,

Food for the Hungry, World Vision, Pugwash International, Lawyers for Social Responsibility, Project Ploughshares, World Federalists, Physicians for Global Survival and many others. Their growing effectiveness has not been lost on many of the world's states, which have sought to partner with NGOs to further mutual goals. One notable success in this regard was the "Ottawa Process" that culminated in an international convention to ban landmines. This was the result of a partnership between NGOs and governments, led by Canada, which were willing to acknowledge the awful consequences for civilians of these weapons.

Nuclear weapons also threaten terrible consequences for humanity, and momentum is building to renew efforts aimed at their elimination. Many governments are beginning to recognize the interests of their populations in nuclear disarmament. The New Agenda Coalition, made up of seven countries (Brazil, Egypt, Ireland, Mexico, New Zealand, South Africa and Sweden), has introduced annual resolutions at the UN General Assembly calling for general and complete nuclear disarmament and a reduction of strategic nuclear arsenals.

International support for these resolutions has been strong: in 2003, 133 states voted in favor of the omnibus resolution, while 6 voted against and 38 abstained. Those states that voted against the resolution (France, India, Pakistan, Israel, the U.K., and the U.S.) all have existing or suspected nuclear programs. Among the states that abstained were all the remaining members of NATO, with the sole exception of Canada. Canada's decision to support the NAC resolution in 2002 and 2003 is significant, given NATO's insistence on a continuing role for nuclear weapons in its defense policy, and the deployment of nuclear weapons on the territory of several non-nuclear NATO member states. Canada's support will enable pressure from civil society groups on the remaining NATO hold-outs to be more effective, and my hope is that ongoing efforts by NGOs such as the Middle Powers Initiative will eventually succeed in persuading other NATO states to realize the urgent need for concrete movement toward nuclear disarmament.

The Involvement of Youth

While civil society has had as yet only limited success in pushing for increased security for humanity, it is the limitless potential of concerted action by people around the world that is a cause for hope for the future. In the lead-up to the U.S. invasion of Iraq, millions of people around the world protested American intentions by taking to the streets. Students were a significant presence in these protests; in the U.S., thousands walked out of classes in over 300 schools across the country, using the slogan "Books not Bombs" to express their opposition to the war.

Many NGOs, including Pugwash and Amnesty International, have youth wings that provide a forum for interested students to learn more about peace and development issues and to translate their knowledge into action. Amnesty's youth membership numbers over 500,000 people worldwide, including nearly 400 youth groups in Canada, and each year they undertake a National Week of Student Action, focusing international attention on an important global issue; in 2003, it was the AIDS pandemic, and this year they will raise awareness about violence against women. International Student/Young Pugwash is currently formulating recommendations for reform of the United Nations, and is also involved in the campaign against weapons in space.

Youth also have a significant stake in the fate of nuclear weapons, which threaten to bring an untimely end to their world. In fact, it is the youth of today that hold the balance of future nuclear policy in their hands. If the youth insist on claiming what is their basic human right to peace, and refuse to be satisfied with anything less than the comprehensive elimination of nuclear weapons, then there is no government or military that will be able to stand in their way. This is true in part because of the growing power of civil society groups, which welcome the energetic participation of youth. But it is also a result of the fact that the leaders of tomorrow will themselves be drawn from the youth of today. It is this that gives me hope for the 21st century, in spite of the ongoing threat posed by nuclear weapons.

FAITH, HOPE AND CHARITY
Reverend Theodore M. Hesburgh

*T*here is little hope for men and women in the future unless we can cultivate those wonderful theological virtues of faith, hope and charity, which not only bind us to God but also give us the highest dimension in which we can work for a better world and especially for peace.

There is not much agreement about what is meant by those three words of faith, hope and charity, even though they are the theological virtues that bring us to God.

The Importance of Faith

Faith is a good place to begin because there cannot be any better future unless we have faith in our ability to work with God to create a better world, with values that are not merely temporal but eternal. It is not easy to have this kind of faith because it is like groping in the dark, not quite knowing what we shall find. However, faith tells us that we find God and that means a sense of order and coherence in our universe. I'd rather not create a chaos on earth, but a place in which humanity can work to create a better world than the one that now exists.

To me that means that with faith we can create the world of values, the greatest of which is peace. Peace is not exactly an easy commodity in today's world. We know that no peace is possible without order. Order in this sense means that we respect human dignity, the opportunity of humans to create a better world than that in which they find themselves. Faith leads us to think about this better world and what might be done to create it.

I think the first thing that comes to mind is justice which is the way to peace in human society. There is an old Latin proverb, *opus justitiae pax*. There can be no peace without justice and one would conclude that at present we are living in a very unjust world, in which powerful people dominate less powerful people and exploit them for their own personal selfish good. In an unjust world, one must begin to work for the kind of justice that is good for everyone, no matter what their status in life or their hopes for the future. With justice, we simply say that every person should have a chance to work for those goals which are most desirable. Among the highest of these is peace in this world, without which nothing stable is accomplished or maintained.

All of this leads us into a contemplation of violence and injustice which always seems to be at the root of an unstable world, without much hope for the future. To the extent that all of us can work for justice in our particular society and then, more broadly, justice towards the whole world, we have a chance of achieving peace in our times. Peace is more than the absence of violence. It presumes that we create a world order in which every person has a chance to achieve as much as every other person, in which education is a fact of life available to everyone who desires it. Peace is not something we simply inherit, but is something we work for by trying to achieve peace in our times. Again, in a kind of circular argument, that is not possible without working for justice since peace is the work of justice and nothing else. It takes a good deal of faith to believe that all of this is possible, and that working together, as persons of good will in this world, we might achieve a measure of justice for everyone which will eventually lead to peace in the world.

To the extent that we promote injustice or at least allow it to happen, we simply are not peacemakers.

The Virtues of Hope and Love

The next great theological virtue is hope. What I have said thus far will never be achieved unless we have firm hope that it is possible. This means that we must embrace every possible means of achieving justice in our times, buoyed up by the hope that it is possible and that it can be done if enough people of good will engage in the enterprise. Hope is a very important component of human life because without it we simply wouldn't have the will to try to achieve what faith makes possible.

The last theological virtue, and the most important is love, or theologically speaking, charity. Love cannot be viewed as this silly sentimental thing but a strong force that leads us to walk the path of justice buoyed up by our hope. None of the schemes for a world of peace will amount to anything unless our efforts are inspired by the love of God, the love of our fellow human beings, and the love of peace to which we all aspire.

Love is the mother of heroism and heroism indeed is what is needed in today's world, with all of its complications, all of its hatreds, and all of its injustices. One might well ask the question: is all of this an illusion, a pipedream? Here again, we need to be buoyed by faith and hope if we are to do the work of love, which is to achieve peace in our times, diminution of violence, a steady work towards human order in the face of worldwide disorder, and a championing of justice in a world that is largely unjust and violent.

Having voiced this dream, one must ask: Is it possible? I do not think it is possible without supernatural help, a calling on the power of prayer, dedicating ourselves in our deepest commitment to become people of peace, not people of violence or injustice. Is this an impossible dream? I think not. If we ponder the stakes in a world without faith, hope and love, it would indeed be a sad world, a bleak world, and a world of violence, injustice and war. Unless we are willing to accept that kind of world, then I think we must all commit ourselves to lives of faith, hope and love.

This calls for a deep commitment, a great imagination regarding how faith, hope and love are possible in our times. It means looking closely at structures that bind us together, the laws that maintain order in the world, the abhorrence of violence in all of its forms, and a complete disavowal of hatred in any of its hideous manifestations.

When all of this is said, it simply means that we must love each other. We must have faith in a possible new future and hope that all of this is possible if we are deeply motivated by faith, hope and love.

THE FLAME OF HOPE

Adam Curle

If we are to tackle constructively the cruel and formidable obstacles to world peace, we must begin by recognizing the elements of the situation for which we, members of the rich and powerful societies, are so largely responsible.

In the pre-World War period, I had a couple of carefree years wandering around an area of the Middle East which my ignorance then saw as idyllic, but which now is engulfed in great violence and awesome destruction. Then came World War II, launched by Hitler. I served for five years as a British soldier.

Since then, I was drawn first into work of rehabilitation of those traumatized by war-time experiences, and by the end of the 1950s decade was sucked into the struggle to build peace. This has lasted until now. I was deeply and personally involved in seeking peace in a number of wars in Africa, Asia and finally Europe, several of these commitments lasting for up to five years. I worked variously with the heads of governments, with rebel leaders, and with ordinary citizens to find ways of escape from the murderous trap of war.

Intensifying Conflict

About halfway through this period, I remember saying that it seemed to me that what we used to call civil wars—often small to start with, but unspeakably vicious—were becoming more common and more desperate, more cruel and often more obviously pointless. My colleagues agreed; this was also their impression. But, the conflicts were also lasting longer and growing more extensive.

I mention this slice of autobiography as a piece of my personal evidence, namely that the many poorer nations had very good cause for complaint against the wealthier ones. And I can also support the second piece of evidence for which there is ample proof in the form of well-documented famines, epidemics, poverty and general under-development of the "developing" world, despite and often because of our national and grandiosely fraudulent international trading and aid institutions. Their wealthy "supporters" (despite some exceptions—and many riots!) maintain to this day a stranglehold on the poor nations.

Added to the burden of callous, uncaring and sporadic stewardship of the natural world, we must list some of the specific pains we have inflicted: exorbitant use of oil, global warming, and the growing shortage of water, among others. This last is partly due to destruction of the rain forests for non-essential timber, and has led to the extinction of so much fish and wildlife. All this contributes to an arid world which we deplore and mourn.

And now we come to the greatest act of collective damage: the Third World War, now beginning between the rich countries and the poor, the "Democracies" and the "Evil Terrorists." The longer this conflict lasts, of course, and the more viciously it is waged, the more difficult becomes contact or rapport, let alone reconciliation between the two main hostile parties.

Moving Toward Peace

These, then, are the main obstacles to even the most tentative hint at negotiations, let alone peace, between the two larger blocks. Indeed, it may be assumed that any tentative move towards rapprochement is likely to be considered—initially at least—as a weakening of resolve (or indeed, as treachery). Neither side can move in this direction except by reducing its hostile stance to an extent that would simply encourage more intense aggression.

The first step is to find, if they do not present themselves, and to encourage the *right people on both sides* to take on the job. They will meet dislike and suspicion; they must even be prepared to die. There are no awards, financial or prestigious—more likely the opposite; no powerful position to enhance the ego. They must be shrewd and well informed. They must be ready to work quietly on their own.

The probably unwilling "hosts" of these often clandestine emissaries will also have hard words from their own side. What are these messengers up to, what is their game?

And who should do it? We—the concerned people—should make the initial contact. We should propose mixed teams to tackle particular problems. With progress in reciprocal sympathy and understanding, it is to be hoped—even expected—that a path towards stable peace will become generally accepted.

It is hardly to be expected that progress will be assured. The route will be mined at every point. Every step forward will be perilous and could be catastrophic.

But with courage and good will, the journey will be possible and the path will be passable. We must never falter for fear of failure, nor dowse the flame of hope.

HOPE IN THE POWER OF NONVIOLENT LOVE

Mairead Corrigan Maguire

On 11th September, people everywhere were shocked into the realization that we live in a dangerous world. Those who lost loved ones, and the American people, had our sympathy. But how did the American Administration respond? Tragically, very badly. There was no breath of vision, no wisdom, only violence, terror, and war. In spite of millions of people calling for "no war," British and American Forces rained death and destruction on the people of Afghanistan and then Iraq. Iraq, a country where, when I visited in 1999, not only their children, but the whole country, was being destroyed by the effects of the Gulf War, economic sanctions of UN/USA/UK, and the cruelty of a military dictator. As if their lives were not desperate enough, they were brutally bombed again. These wars were not heroic, courageous, or honorable. They were immoral, illegal, and unnecessary. In time, all those involved in the murder of many thousands of Iraqi people (the latest figure is more than 100,000 civilians) and Afghans will want to say they are sorry. Over 1,000 US and many British soldiers were killed, and untold thousands of US soldiers injured.

The Russian war against Chechnya was another example of state terror against a civilian population. This planted seeds of revenge and hatred, and resulted in desperate acts of terrorism, such as those against the children of Beslan. As sure as Spring follows Winter, terrorism follows state violence and repression. In spite of this, we are promised ongoing wars by the United States. I believe that war is State terrorism by another name, and is itself a threat to humankind. It may well be only a matter of time before some government or terrorist group decides to use nuclear weapons, and that is why nuclear proliferation is also a threat.

Abolishing War

We must do all in our power, through the United Nations, to abolish war, and make it illegal under International Law. The US is a superpower, but we the people of the world, when united, are a stronger Superpower, because we state a truth that "every human life is sacred and we should not be killing each other in violence, ethnic conflicts, and war." It is time now for the United Nations to recover the mantle of responsibility and authority that has been unfortunately usurped by the United States; the people of the world demand this as our right.

Violence and war are immoral and are not an acceptable way of solving the problems of the human family. There are alternatives. In the past, in response to injustice, we had two choices, fight or flight; but there is a third way, the way of non-violence. This way was open to the political leaders of Britain and America, but they chose the old way of war. The world was taken to war under false pretenses. There were no weapons of mass destruction, and it was only a matter of time before the people of Iraq would have changed their regime. There was no political will to solve the problems nonviolently, but only a military mindset steeped in the fantasy that might is right, and war works! How sad that, amongst many people, the moral authority of both US and Britain has been lost, as has trust in both countries' political leadership. We need political leaders with vision, who are trusted, and have the ability to give people hope and confidence in themselves and others, belief that they matter and can make a difference.

September 11th raises many questions. What motivated those who carried out this cruel and inhumane attack? In order to deal with insurgency violence, we need to understand the psychology behind such violence. We humans share the same basic human nature. We have an innate sense of justice. We feel injustice deeply; it can make us fearful, angry, and frustrated. We each have a war of emotions going on in our hearts. If injustice is constant, severe, and unrelenting, with no avenue of redress, it can bring about a violent, explosive, even murderous response. We are each murderous, given the right circumstances, and that is why we need to teach nonviolence, and methods such as meditation to help us deal with our emotions; as well as strategies which work to deal with the injustices. I lived this experience myself, in "the troubles" in Northern Ireland. Witnessing State violence and injustice, I understand how people can react with violence, often seeing it as an alternative to doing nothing.

It is important that we do not demonize, dehumanize, or underestimate the commitment to justice held by those who choose the "armed struggle" as a way of change. But it is equally important that we do not glorify violence, make heroes of those who use violence, or be ambiguous about the use of violence. Such ambiguity often leaves people (who themselves are trapped in an unjust, violent, emotional, politically charged situation) confused about the use of violence.

In Northern Ireland the "armed struggle" was engaged in and supported by some as a reaction to State injustice and violence, and by others for their own political agenda. Some political activists argued the phony theory of "Just War" in a misguided attempt to give religious credence to their use of violence. The "armed struggle" appealed to some as heroic and gave them a role of authority and power in an otherwise bleak and hopeless situation. In the height of their inner emotional war and outer societal war, it was easy for people to get caught up into violent revolutionary zeal and fervor. They argued any means justified the end, even dying on hunger strikes for their political cause. In Northern Ireland, the "Hunger Strikes to the Death" were, I believe, wrong. Palestinian Suicide bombers are, I believe, wrong. The lives of Hunger Strikers and Suicide Bombers are sacred, as are the lives of all others. Whilst I understand what drives people to such violent actions often in an attempt to call attention to injustices, if we want justice, we must use just means to attain it.

Nonviolent Resistance

By using Nonviolent Resistance (which we all must do when faced with injustice) we acknowledge both our own humanness and the humanness of opponents. Nonviolent Resistance opens the possibility for people to change. I have come to believe that the only hope for real change is when we the human family refuse to hurt or kill each other, and begin to build non-killing societies and a non-killing world. By totally rejecting violence and killing as inhumane and unacceptable and solving our problems by peaceful means, we will be living out of the true spirit of our human nature, and we will be happy. This is possible, and it starts with each one of us, seeking truth and living our lives with as much integrity as possible.

Governments have a responsibility to use means consistent with their ends that uphold ethical policies, and the highest standards of justice, human rights. They must also recognize the right to nonviolent dissent, and open channels of communications so that all grievances can be addressed. The new US doctrine of war without end, i.e. "war on terrorism," is itself creating a climate of fear and hatred. "War on terrorism" is also a myth, as there is no such thing as a war without an enemy. Terrorism is a tactic, not an enemy. The problem is one of small but growing cells of people in various countries using violence, in a misguided attempt to right wrongs. They have deep grievances, which must be addressed politically. They cannot be solved militarily. In Northern Ireland, there was and is a recognition that militarism, paramilitarism, and emergency laws are counter-productive, and that the only way forward is to deal with the root cause of the conflict, through all-inclusive dialogue. Thus began the process of dialogue with paramilitary representatives, demilitarization, and a peace process. As part of this conflict resolution process, we were encouraged by the Irish, British and American political leadership to negotiate with representatives of Paramilitary Organizations. There are lessons to be learned from the conflict resolution process in Northern Ireland, including the need to talk to the terrorists or their political representatives.

Justice and Human Rights

We can increase our security by States implementing the highest standards of Justice and Human Rights, and implementing law built on the principles of the universality of human nature. When government laws respect people, people will respect the law. Also, international co-operation and outreach to other countries will help stop violence. But most important is dealing with the root causes of violent conflict, and taking the guns out of the situation, so people can begin to build peace across the ground.

A key factor in stopping insurgency in the Middle East is the necessity of a genuine Peace Process. I am inspired and take hope from the Israeli/Palestinian peace movement. I believe every help should be given to them and the civil community, as their efforts are necessary to build trust and peace on the ground. The international community is concerned about the injustice against the Palestinian people by the Israeli government. Demolition of homes, building of the wall, and the military repression suffered daily by Palestinian people is cruel, inhumane, and breaks international law. The occupation is wrong. Such Israeli State violence and injustices lead to suicide bombings, which also are a cruel and counterproductive method of resistance. The Israeli people will never know safety and security, until they make justice and peace with their Palestinian, Iraqi, Syrian and Iranian neighbors. The international community must implement economic and political actions against Israel until a genuine peace agreement with Palestinian leaders is in process.

We hear talk about a clash of civilizations. I do not believe this and I think we have to stand against those who, for their own agenda, try to whip up enmity between people and nations.

The Irish poet, William Butler Yeats, wrote:

"We had fed the heart on fantasies,
The hearts' grown brutal from the fare;
More substance in our enmities
Than in our love."
                    -The Stare's Nest by My Window

For a new generation, a new age, we must use our love to overcome the fear and enmities of past generations. I am full of hope, because I believe in people, and I believe passionately in the power of nonviolent love to build a unified world civilization with a heart.

HOPE FROM ASHES

Dennis Rivers

*E*very August 6th the extended community of the Nuclear Age Peace Foundation gathers, as do people around the world, to mark the deaths and injuries of the inhabitants of the cities of Hiroshima and Nagasaki. Death in war is horrible to contemplate even when all the participants are willing combatants. The victims of the first atomic bomb attacks were, to a large degree, children, women and non-combatants, which makes this particular episode in American history even more difficult to think about. In spite of the passing of more than half a century, some Americans are still unreconciled to the tragic events of World War II, and especially to those of August, 1945. Still unreconciled, because so many still believe that America was right to use nuclear weapons in 1945 and is right to build more of them today: new ones, better ones, the final solution to all that threatens us in a threatening world!

Over many years of August 6th memorials I have asked myself the question, What could we learn from this painful issue, that might prevent us from creating new tragedies? In that question I find hope, although it is a hope heavily surrounded with warnings.

The aspect of World War II that I find most disturbing is that, as concerns the methods of war, Hitler won World War II. The war was portrayed at the time by the Allied powers as a conflict over high principles, a conflict of decency and democracy against tyranny and evil. But although the Allies won the war in some ways, sober reflection suggests that they lost the war in others. In the end one of Hitler's most important principles prevailed: the mass murder of civilians in order to achieve military and/or political goals. Early in the war Hitler began gassing, incinerating or otherwise killing large numbers of civilians. By the end of the war American and British air forces were fully engaged in the mass murder of civilians through the fire-bombing of entire cities. That this fire-bombing campaign began as righteous revenge for Hitler's air raids against British cities only demonstrates how quickly the participants in war can come to resemble one another.

Hiroshima and Nagasaki

The atom-bombing of Hiroshima and Nagasaki represented a stunning leap forward in the technology of murder by fire and radiation poisoning. By August, 1945, massive fire-bombing air raids had already burned sixty-six of Japan's largest cities to the ground.[1] But these raids required thousands of planes and days of conflagration. Now it could be done in a moment, with a single B-29: a portable Auschwitz that the United States could inflict on anyone, anywhere.

Well, you may say, that was half a century ago. Why should we continue to think about these tragic and unfortunate events when there are plenty of current tragedies to lament?

For me, the answer is that we Americans have still not acknowledged our capacity for mass murder, which we continue to euphemize and depersonalize with such terms as "collateral damage." Collateral damage consists of all the people we have killed or injured, whom we did not particularly intend to kill or maim, but who just happened to be in the way, and whose presence we have consistently refused to acknowledge. There were millions of such casualties in Japan, millions more in

Vietnam and who knows how many in Korea, Iraq and so on. It seems to me, as an American, that Americans have taken the moral principle that *intentions matter* and applied it mind-numbingly backwards. Since we can tell ourselves that we did not specifically intend to kill these many persons, the tragedy of their deaths does not seem to matter to us. What disturbs me most here is the ease with which we close our eyes to *not see* those whom we have injured, wronged, killed.

The Technologization of Violence

The technologization of violence plays a key role in making these victims invisible. High technology weapons intoxicate their possessors with God-like powers of destruction, distract their possessors with the complex details of their operation, and remove their possessors from the scenes of injury and death. Thus, for decades the United States, from a giant, electronics-packed bunker carved into a mountain, has targeted its complex and all-powerful missiles on various military installations in what was the Soviet Union, willfully ignoring the fact that a nuclear strike on those targets would result in the death by incineration and radiation poisoning of millions of nearby civilians. It just did not seem to matter. A more recent example concerns depleted uranium. Depleted uranium is a metal so hard that it cuts through tank armor and reinforced concrete like a knife cutting through an apple (and burns to a fine dust while doing so). Thrilled by our success in making perfect anti-tank and "bunker-buster" weapons, we have used depleted uranium munitions in all our recent conflicts, and have left spread across the lands of Kosovo, Afghanistan and Iraq a layer of uranium dust that will be both poisonous and radioactive to all the inhabitants of those lands and all their descendants for the next five billion years. Tell me, then: Although we had the Nuremberg war crimes trials, and announced fine principles about not injuring civilians, whose rules of war prevailed after World War II? Ours, or Hitler's?

If a team of evil geniuses had come to Harry Truman in August of 1945 with a dozen Japanese babies and a blowtorch, and said, "Mr. President, just take this blowtorch in your hands and burn these infants to death one at a time, live on worldwide radio, and we guarantee that the Japanese will surrender right away," Truman, I'm sure, would have turned away in disgust. But, under the multiple spells of revenge, racism, weapons-intoxication, and self-deceiving abstractions like "the enemy" and "military target," Harry Truman and his earnest, sober colleagues consigned thousands of infants and children to their fiery deaths. ("To avoid a bloody invasion of Japan," some say, even to this day, perhaps not realizing the grisly pragmatism they are espousing: kill the children and you can bend the adults to your will.)[2]

Unfortunately, the same hypnotic spells and fevered rationalizations that led to the first use of nuclear weapons continue to circulate in the collective psyche of the entire world, tempting people everywhere to try to resolve their conflicts or defend their interests with the latest whiz-bang, laser-blinding death ray, land mine, Stealth fighter, poison gas or supposed "smart bomb," never mind who's down there on the ground. Mechanized violence is a sort of underground religion of the twentieth century, a cult of the explosion, worshipped in a thousand movies and ritually enacted each day by millions of video game players exulting in virtual mayhem.

Not a year goes by in the United States without some group within the military-industrial complex proposing yet a new generation of nuclear weapons, some new design that will finally keep us safe, finally obliterate our enemies. When one considers that six trillion dollars spent over sixty years on nuclear weapons and their delivery systems have still not made America safe, one would be forced to conclude, I believe, that there are some deeply irrational thought processes going on here. Paradoxically, admitting that our defense planners are irrational about nuclear weapons would be a truly significant step toward sanity. (Some courageous military officers have taken exactly that step.)

Acknowledging Our Vulnerability

Only by acknowledging how vulnerable we *all* are to these murderous enthusiasms, confusions, self-numbings, self-deceptions, and fantasies of infinite power, to which the souls of the Hiroshima and Nagasaki dead bear silent witness, can we avoid repeating the moral catastrophes of our past and present.

Why remember Hiroshima and Nagasaki? If the memory of those who suffered there continues to remind us of how easily we can slip into the blind trance of violence, then those who suffered may yet save the lives of innumerable others, perhaps even our own lives. Although the events of August 1945 cannot be changed, the lessons we learn from those events can continue to evolve over many decades and centuries.

Hope from ashes.

---

[1] For a review of the firebombing of Japanese cities in World War II, see Kenneth P. Werrell, *Blankets of Fire: U.S. Bombers over Japan in World War II*. Washington: Smithsonian Institution Press. 1996.

[2] For a review of the rationales invoked to justify the use of the atomic bomb, see Gar Aperovitz, *The Decision to Use the Atomic Bomb*. London: Harper-Collins. 1995.

FIFTY-ONE REASONS FOR HOPE

David Krieger

1. Each new dawn.
2. The miracle of birth.
3. Our capacity to love.
4. The courage of nonviolence.
5. Gandhi, King and Mandela.
6. The night sky.
7. Spring.
8. Flowers and bees.
9. The arc of justice.
10. Whistleblowers.
11. Butterflies.
12. The full moon.
13. Teachers.
14. Simple wisdom.
15. Dogs and cats.
16. Friendship.
17. Our ability to reflect.
18. Our capacity for joy.
19. The Dalai Lama, Desmond Tutu and Oscar Romero.
20. The gift of conscience.
21. Human rights and responsibilities.
22. Our capacity to nurture.
23. The ascendancy of women.
24. Innocence.

25. Our capacity to change.
26. Mozart, Beethoven and Chopin.
27. The internet.
28. War resisters.
29. Everyday heroes.
30. Lions, tigers, bears, elephants and giraffes.
31. Conscientious objectors.
32. Tolstoy, Twain and Vonnegut.
33. Wilderness.
34. Our water planet.
35. Solar energy.
36. Picasso, Matisse and Miro.
37. World citizens.
38. Life.
39. The survivors of Hiroshima and Nagasaki.
40. The King of Hearts.
41. Rain.
42. Sunshine.
43. Pablo Neruda.
44. Grandchildren.
45. Mountains.
46. Sunflowers.
47. The Principles of Nuremberg.
48. A child's smile.
49. Dolphins.
50. Wildflowers.
51. Our ability to choose hope.

Wage
Peace

"Peace can only last where human rights are respected, where people are fed, and where individuals and nations are free."

– The XIVth Dalai Lama

"Peace cannot be kept by force. It can only be achieved by understanding."

– Albert Einstein

"One day we must come to see that peace is not merely a distant goal that we seek, but that it is a means by which we arrive at that goal. We must pursue peaceful ends through peaceful means."

– Martin Luther King, Jr.

THE CHALLENGE OF PEACE

David Krieger

There is a Roman dictum, "If you want peace, prepare for war." This has been diligently followed for over 2,000 years. It has always resulted in more war. We need a new dictum: "If you want peace, prepare for peace." This is a critical challenge of the Nuclear Age. In considering this challenge, I will discuss below: perspective, education, appreciation, choice and engagement. Taken together, I believe they make a compelling argument that each of us is needed to achieve the challenge of peace.

Perspective

The Nuclear Age began only 60 years ago, a mere nano-second in geological time. Scientists tell us that the universe began 15 billion years ago, in the immensely distant past. We can conceive of the life of the universe as a 15,000-page book, with each page representing a million years. In this book, the "Big Bang" would occur at the beginning of page one and then thousands of pages would represent the expansion of the universe and the creation of stars. The Earth would have been formed around page 10,500. The beginning of life on Earth, the first single-celled creatures, would have occurred on about page 11,000. And then over the next 4,000 pages, you could read about life developing. Only three pages from the end of this 15,000 page book would our human ancestors appear. It would not be until the last word on the last page of the book that human civilizations would appear. The Nuclear Age would fall in the period—the punctuation mark—of the last sentence of the last page of the history of the universe.

So, in the development of the universe, of all that has preceded us in time and on this planet, the Nuclear Age is infinitesimally tiny, and yet it is incredibly important, for it is the funnel through which we must pass to move into the future. For the first time in history, a species, our own, has developed technology capable of destroying itself and most of life on the planet.

We need this perspective of our place in time and the history of the universe to more fully appreciate how extraordinarily rare and precious life is in general and each of us is in particular.

Education

We are all born as blank slates. Our minds are unformed and uninformed. It is only by education that we develop our views and prejudices. It is only by education that we draw boundaries with their inclusions and exclusions. Education shapes our view of the world. We can educate in our families, schools, communities and other societal institutions for peace or for war. We can educate to create critical thinkers or to create individuals who will charge into battle or support wars without thinking. Our education largely determines our willingness to fight in wars (or to send others to fight), or to fight for peace.

At the outset of the Nuclear Age, Albert Einstein, the greatest scientist of the 20th century, observed, "The splitting of the atom has changed everything save our modes of thinking and thus we drift toward unparalleled catastrophe." If we are to avoid this "unparalleled catastrophe," which continues to threaten us, we must educate ourselves and in turn educate others about upholding human dignity for all and finding alternatives to violence. It is helpful in this sense to look to the lives of great peace heroes, such as Mahatma Gandhi, Martin Luther King, Jr., Nelson Mandela and the Dalai Lama.

We must also educate for global citizenship, for the shared responsibility of passing on the planet and its life forms intact to the next generation. Arundhati Roy, the great Indian writer and activist, has said this about nuclear weapons, whether or not they're used: "They violate everything that is humane; they alter the meaning of life. Why do we tolerate them? Why do we tolerate the men who use nuclear weapons to blackmail the human race?" It is a question of education. These men and these weapons should not be tolerated.

Appreciation

We live in an amazingly beautiful world, and each of us is a miracle. Have you ever stopped to consider what a miracle you are? All the things that we take for granted are such miracles: that we can see this beautiful earth, its trees and streams and flowers; that we can hear songs; that we have voices to speak and sing; that we can communicate with each other; that we can form relationships and can love and cherish each other; that we can work and play; that we can walk and run and skip; that we can breathe and do all the incredible things we take for granted. If we can learn to appreciate how miraculous we truly are, perhaps we can also appreciate that each of us is equally a miracle. How can one miracle wish to injure or kill another? The gift of life must be rooted in appreciation, which gives rise to compassion and empathy.

Choice

We all make choices about what we do with our lives. We can devote our lives to a focus on accumulation of material things, which is culturally acceptable, or we can set our sights on fulfilling more compassionate goals aimed at building a peaceful world.

The Earth Charter, a wonderful document that was created with input from people all over the world and issued in the year 2000, begins with these words: "We stand at a critical moment in Earth's history, a time when humanity must choose its future." But humanity will not choose by a vote. The choice will be made by the individual choices of each of us. Each choice matters.

The Earth Charter further states: "The choice is ours: form a global partnership to care for Earth and one another or risk the destruction of ourselves and the diversity of life."

In 1955, Albert Einstein, the great scientist, and Bertrand Russell, a leading 20th century philosopher and mathematician, issued a manifesto in which they concluded: "There lies before us, if we choose, continual progress in happiness, knowledge and wisdom. Shall we, instead, choose death, because we cannot forget our quarrels? We appeal as human beings to human beings: Remember your humanity, and forget the rest. If you can do so, the way lies open to a new Paradise; if you cannot, there lies before you the risk of universal death."

The two most powerful images that emerged from the 20th century were the mushroom cloud from a nuclear explosion and the view of Earth looking back from outer space. The mushroom cloud represents universal destruction, while the view of Earth from space represents the unique and solitary beauty of our planet, the only planet we know of that harbors life, in a vast, dark universe. These images represent polar opposite possibilities for humanity's future. Which will we choose?

We each have the power of choice.

Engagement

We need to become personally involved in the issues of our time, and find our own ways to work for a peaceful future. Among the important ways in which we can engage are by speaking out and making our presence felt for a peaceful world. That means opposing policies of violence and war. It means standing up for the human dignity of everyone, everywhere. We must create a world that works for all and we must begin where we are, but our vision and our outreach must be global. We must demand more of our leaders, and we must choose better leaders. We ourselves must become the leaders who will change the world. The most important change has always come from below and from outside the power structure.

We must become world citizens. This means citizens of a polity that does not yet exist. By our commitment and our vision we can create the structures and institutions that will in time give rise to a Federation of the Peoples of Earth. We must ultimately transform the United Nations into such a federation and, more immediately, give life to the International Criminal Court, which will hold all leaders accountable for genocide, crimes against humanity and war crimes.

To fight for peace is to fight for life and the future of our species and our planet. Our engagement and our endurance are essential to our human survival.

My Hope for You

My hope for you is that you will choose peace in all of its dimensions.

You can begin by choosing hope. It is your belief that you *can* make a difference that will allow you to do so. Put aside despair, apathy, complacency and ignorance, and instead choose hope. It is the first step on the path to peace.

Saint Augustine said, "Hope has two beautiful daughters: anger and courage; anger at the way things are, and courage to change them." There is virtue in anger against injustice and you will certainly need courage to be a non-violent warrior for peace.

You are needed in the struggle for the triumph of humanity over violence, war, and weapons of weapons of mass destruction. May you be bold, creative and persistent in your efforts. May you rise to your full stature of human dignity to meet the challenge of peace.

THE BUSINESS OF PEACE
Dame Anita Roddick

Look at the role of business in the world today and you'll see how wars happen. But I've spent the last 29 years with my company, The Body Shop, trying to exemplify the ways in which business can and must be a force for positive change, for stability and, therefore, for peace.

I've seen how business crosses borders and how trade knows no difference between peace and war. I've seen how the corporations who control that trade have acquired the power to decide between war and peace. Business doesn't get much bigger than that. Half of the world's biggest economies are corporations. But businesses are not found in nature—they are created by humans and are therefore subject to the changes that humans can impose on them. So as long as we can put some idealism back on the global agenda, there is still a light at the end of the tunnel.

Whether we're talking about Shell or Nestlé, all types of multinational corporations benefit by escaping national restrictions on their activities. With greater ability to move their operations and capital around the world, companies can pick and choose which laws they operate under and have greater influence with national governments than ever before.

Business Is Not Neutral

Business is not apolitical or neutral on the international agenda. It has consistently argued the case for a laissez-faire agenda of deregulation and globalization. In doing so, it has increasingly marginalized communities and sown the seeds of conflict while it has directly benefited as a result. In case after case where commercial and human-rights interests compete for attention, you can bet your bottom dollar that commerce prevails.

But when the product is weaponry, designed and built for the sole purpose of killing people, this becomes even more critical. That's why the growth of the arms industry offers a particularly graphic paradigm of the dangers of globalization.

North America and Western Europe account for well over half of all of the military spending worldwide today. That's how economic concerns become the driving force behind arms policies and take precedence over human rights abuses, where profits are more aligned with private greed than public good.

When weapons are sold, there is an endorsement implicit in the provision of one set of people with the equipment to kill another: we support your use of deadly force to achieve your aims. There is great motivation for the companies to perpetuate themselves and this situation. And if they've got the weapons, they've also got access to ministers and top-level military information, which in turn grants influence over national and global defense policy. Then, when arms companies begin to operate outside of national boundaries, they can play military powers against one another. Hence their control over war and peace.

Arms makers have managed to convince government after government that the way to keep their domestic economies from withering is to sell more weapons abroad—especially to developing countries, where most conflicts now occur. Sales beyond "the West"—in Asia, Africa, the Middle East and Latin America—are seen as crucial to the industry; the bread and butter deals. They have the longer production runs, the lower development costs and the inflated prices that are not present in NATO deals.

It is in the regions of tension and conflict zones, regional arms races and highly militarized, usually human-rights abusing states, that there is greatest demand for weapons or opportunity to create that demand. Most armed conflicts today—including a significant aspect of the unrest in Iraq and Afghanistan stemming from the invasions—are internal wars and 90% of the casualties are civilians. Even where armed conflict is avoided, military priorities deprive the local population of the benefits of potential spending on human development. Some of the poorest countries spend more on their military than on their people's education, health, and the care that a decent human life encompasses. Unchecked, a situation like this breeds conditions that sooner or later are likely to provoke popular insurrections. Over and over again, we see private greed taking precedence over public good.

It's a high-stakes industry. Single deals can make or break companies. At its height, the notorious Al Yamamah deal with Saudi Arabia accounted for over 75% of all UK arms exports on its own. This explains the enormous push to get big package deals (often with massive government backing and incentives like off-set deals), commission payments and licensed production. Licensed production is where equipment is partially or completely manufactured in the buyer country. This ranges from using a guaranteed amount of locally sourced components to the entire production taking place in the buyer country with just the technical means and know-how supplied. This allows vendors to benefit from cheap labor and low labor and industrial standards. And, by buying stakes in these local companies as part of deals or in parallel with sales, or merging with them to produce hybrids, the multi-national players have evolved into enormously powerful and complex international networks.

The Blind Pursuit of Free Trade

According to the theory some call free trade, we should all be happy that the globe is rapidly becoming a playground for those who can move capital and projects quickly from place to place. We business people, according to this theory, will make everyone better off if we can roam from country to country with no restrictions—in search of the lowest wages, the loosest environmental regulations, and the most docile and desperate workers. Ah yes, many would say—but free trade brings growth and jobs. That is the rub. I do not believe that unfettered free trade inevitably brings growth in anything but short-term profits and long-term environmental destruction.

I believe those who are now in control—the economic governments, politicians and business people—could drive us off the edge. Global planning institutions like the World Bank, the IMF and especially the World Trade Organization are ignoring mounting evidence of impending social catastrophe that will leave widespread and dangerous inequality and insecurity. These institutions aren't working for the majority of humanity. And the roots of conflict aren't found amongst the dispossessed and the poor, but rather, they can be found within our global policies that lead them into retaliation.

It seems to me that as a by-product of economic growth we produce an enemy class in the form of those who are excluded or forced downward. We produce conflict in the forms of increasing crime, violence, drugs and rampant selfishness.

There is always someplace in the world that is a little worse off, where the living conditions are a little more wretched. Just look at industry after industry in search of even lower wages and looser standards. From Europe or the US, to Taiwan to Mexico, each country is just another pit stop in the race to the bottom. The new frontier is China, where wages and environmental standards are still lower and human rights abuses even more sordidly suppressed. The new nomadic capital never sets down roots and never builds communities; it leaves behind toxic wastes and embittered workers.

So if the blind pursuit of free trade continues, political instability will also return big time. The rise of fascism, brutal nationalism, and ethnic racism we see on continent after continent is no accident. Demagogues prey on insecurity and fear. If we do not build an economic paradigm that helps sustain communities, cultures and families, the consequences will be severe.

More and more people are waking up to this truth. It is now business rather than government that is the target of activist groups. Environmental groups are taking on Exxon Oil in the biggest consumer boycott in history. The animal rights movement continues to take on the pharmaceutical, beauty and fashion industries. The human-rights lobby has been joined by ethical investors, vigilante consumers and direct action specialists in targeting the multinationals who are among the biggest contributors to global instability.

In harvesting poor nations' natural resources, multinationals often severely degrade the environment. Additionally, in their eagerness to gain access to Third World resources, multinationals often collaborate with, and support, regimes that brutally repress and steal from their populations.

I've already touched on the arms industry, but just look at the environmental, social and economic impact of oil companies on the Delta region of Nigeria under the Obacha dictatorship. It led to terrible conflicts and thousands lost their lives. The Ogoni people and the other Niger Delta minority communities, like so many other indigenous peoples, were marginalized by the economic and political structures of Nigeria. Money the oil companies paid to the Nigerian government was either spent on military hardware or it left the country to be deposited in Swiss banks. Even post-Obacha, the Ogoni people have still barely benefited from revenues generated by the oil on their lands. And the story of Shell in Ogoniland is scarcely unique. Look at what has been happening with Unocal and Total in Burma.

Business Has Entered Center Stage

Everyone agrees on one important thing: business has entered center stage. It is faster, more creative and wealthier than governments—particularly the governments in developing nations who depend upon its expertise. I accept that you can't stop business from going global, but you can make it listen to the responsibilities that go with that. I don't think that taking responsibility comes from government regulations. It comes from those businesses finally seeing that acting responsibly and responsively (there is a difference) is actually good for business. Business cannot avoid moral choices. Its future depends on it.

For too long, business has been teaching that politics and commerce are two different arenas. They are not. Political awareness and activism must be incorporated into global management. In a global world, there are no value-free or politically disentangled actions; the very act of organizing on a global basis is political because of culture, geography, and differing value systems. Business leaders need to realize this must be the way forward—the personal becomes the political, which becomes the global.

Making Business a Force for Positive Social Change

What I'm saying is that business can and must be a force for positive social change. It must not only avoid hideous evil—it must actively do good.

We need business to be accountable and to base its international behavior on the charters and treaties on sustainability and human rights—so happily signed by governments the world over, but just as easily ignored by them. To be a force for peace, business has to aid the communities in which it operates through positive business practices in the wider social context.

I believe we need a broader model. Call it fair trade, call it sustainable trade, the label does not matter, the content does. We need trade that respects and supports communities and families. We need trade that builds local economic capacities and independence. We need trade that safeguards the environment. We need trade that encourages countries to educate their children, heal their sick, value the work of women and respect human rights. We need to measure progress by human development not gross product.

We need to recognize the rights and contributions of indigenous people who bring vital leadership to the task of conserving the earth and its creatures in creating a new life-affirming global reality. We need to understand that indigenous wisdom constitutes one of human society's most important and irreplaceable resources.

We need to embrace the fact that gender balance is also essential to sustainable development. We need to accept that women's roles, needs, values and wisdom are especially central to decision-making on the fate of the Earth. We need to involve women at all levels of policy-making, planning and implementation on an equal basis with men.

Corporations must start showing more developed emotions than fear and greed and we have to find ways to halt economic growth that alienates non-economic values.

In my company we are always looking for fair trading initiatives with local communities. The Body Shop currently trades directly with 38 communities in need, from 21 countries around the world, many of them primarily benefiting women. By themselves, the initiatives of The Body Shop will not transform the global economy, but they do transform my company's thinking about our responsibility as a business. I would rather be measured by how I treat weaker and frailer communities I trade with than by how great my profits. If all of us in business committed ourselves to such an attitude and such undertakings, big things would indeed happen.

We could keep rural life vital and feasible, rather than watch millions more stream into the squalor of the cities that cannot grow fast enough to keep up. We could help build political stability and sustainable democracy. We could develop a new image and ideal of business that causes less transitional pain and more transformational economic gain.

Business and Peace

So how can business do its bit for peace? Corporate responsibility, plain and simple. We have to rethink our approach to these issues. And then we have to act—in ways big and small—to bring sustainable and healthy growth across the globe. Our political postures must change. We have to stop endlessly whining for easier rules, lower costs, and fewer restrictions. Our business practices must also change. We have to take longer-term views, invest in communities, and build long-lasting markets.

I believe we are some way off from preventing the international conflict created by prevailing business practices, but every bit of pressure helps, from whatever direction—whether it's campaigning for an end to arms, refusing to trade with despots and human rights abusers, finding an alternative to the major economic planning models, setting up small-scale fair trade initiatives, or networking and sharing best practices with socially responsible businesses.

That's what business itself has to do in the interests of global stability and peace.

And you? What's your role in this? How can you do your bit for world peace?

Günther Grass, a novelist who won a Nobel Prize for literature, once said that the job of a citizen is to keep his mouth open. Never stop asking questions. Demand answers. Take it personally. Information is power. You hold the ultimate power over a business' future because you can also hit them where it hurts—in their profit margins. So use your purchasing power wisely. Support those people who are working for change. And never feel that you as an individual can't make all the difference in the world.

HOPE, PEACE AND THE POWER OF YOUNG PEOPLE

Craig and Marc Kielburger

Christine's Story: Hope in a Country Ravaged by War

We first came to know Christine during a trip to war-ravaged Sierra Leone. Like civilians all over the world caught up in armed conflict, she had endured nearly unimaginable suffering. Like so many in her country, she had first-hand experience with the horrors of war. By the time we met, she and her family had been marked by a series of tragedies: the brutal rape of a young niece, the abduction of a nephew and the torture of a brother held in prison. She recounted to us how friends and neighbors had endured similarly appalling acts of violence, often perpetrated by members of their own communities. All too frequently, she told us, atrocities were committed by local children forced to follow orders under threat of death, drugged in order to obediently mutilate and kill. Listening to her story, we silently wondered how she could possibly bear the pain that surrounded her.

We learned that instead of despairing in the face of tragedy, Christine found the courage to respond with resilience, compassion and hope. Under the most difficult of conditions she now works to help those in her community most desperately in need of assistance: children, the aged and the suffering. We soon came to recognize Christine as one of the most generous and vibrant people that we have ever met. When we ventured to ask how she found the strength to help some of the very people who had caused her pain, she told us that although it was far from easy, her own future as well as that of her country depended upon the willingness of ordinary people like herself to act in the spirit of forgiveness and compassion. Christine's devotion to working towards reconciliation and peace in her community and country continues to be an inspiration to us. Her story is a powerful reminder that peace *is* possible, and that it is *made* possible through the efforts of individuals committed to its realization.

The Possibility of Peace, The Power of Youth

Today, there is a widespread tendency to see peace as a distant dream all but lost amid increasing strife. In recent years, we have witnessed both the explosion and escalation of a series of conflicts around the world. These wars often take place within states, and, alarmingly, they are conducted with a callous disregard for human life that makes civilians of all ages popular targets of violence. All too often, the international community has turned a blind eye to the atrocities that have occurred as a result. Meanwhile, cynics and pessimists across the political spectrum proclaim war natural and peace an illusion, loudly lamenting the grim future facing the next generation.

Certainly, the youth of today face profound challenges in a world beset by violence. We have seen that children are particularly affected by the horrors of armed conflict, with entire generations growing up in the midst of violence and destruction. In many places war has become a way of life, and life a desperate battle for survival that many quickly lose. Over the past decade alone, more than two million children have died and six million have been injured as a result of war. Those that survive must bear the moral and spiritual scars of their ordeal in addition to the physical ones. Such scars are a powerful testament to the horrors of war. Yet, we must recognize that in the presence of hope they do not preclude the possibility of peace.

It is now clear that a sustainable peace will never be achieved through simply suppressing conflict. We firmly believe that peace *can* be achieved—through a commitment to breaking the cycle of hatred and violence that sustains war. Thus, it is young people who represent the key to peace, for it is they who are new generation of peace builders. If we are to foster peace, we must begin by investing our time, energy and resources in young people in war-stricken countries such that we encourage them to embrace the virtues of peace and cooperation. The time has come for us to see young people as something more than simply "adults-in-waiting" and instead recognize, empower and celebrate the power of youth to build a peaceful world. Ultimately, children and youth must be recognized as the leaders of today, as well as of tomorrow.

Breaking cycles of violence involves ensuring that children have the chance to grow up secure, in an atmosphere of tolerance, respect and compassion. It means putting an end to deprivation, and the desperation and bitterness it breeds in a world in which only a select few have access to plenty. Beyond this, it requires a commitment to providing children with the opportunity to acquire vital conflict mediation and communication skills, and nurturing their leadership abilities from an early age. This means making it possible for all children to obtain an education. Creating an environment of peace and understanding involves, moreover, a commitment to allowing young people to voice their ideas and concerns in a supportive environment where their contributions are truly valued. With each step that we take to ensure their physical, emotional and spiritual well being, and with each move that we make in support of their peace-building efforts and aspirations, we realize our hopes for a true and lasting peace.

A Network of Children Helping Children

Through our work with Free the Children (FTC), we have had the good fortune to witness the progress that young people are taking to achieve world peace. Founded in 1995, Free the Children is an international network of children helping children engaged in innovative education, peace-building and leadership programming. In our view, all of these realms of activity are intimately connected, and all three are essential to creating a peaceful world. Education and leadership training provide the foundations upon which peace building occurs, and the success of peace-building initiatives provides further opportunities for education and leadership.

Through the hard work and dedication of young people around the world, Free the Children has constructed 400 schools in 21 developing countries, many in war-affected areas. These schools provide children at risk with the skills and knowledge necessary to realize their potential as productive members of their communities. In an effort to promote a broader understanding of the plight of children caught up in violent conflict, Free the Children has entered into a partnership with the United Nations (Office of the Special Representative of the United Nations Secretary General for Children and Armed Conflict) to raise awareness about, and provide educational opportunities to children in war-affected areas. The Youth Ambassadors for Peace initiative mobilizes youth in developed countries on this issue through education, advocacy and action campaigns. Through such efforts, young people in both the developed and developing world are provided with the tools necessary to become the peace builders of both today and tomorrow.

Free the Children's success in both administering major grassroots development projects in many of the poorest and most conflict-ridden regions of the world and implementing effective leadership programs on a global level speaks to the power of children to act as agents of positive change on the largest scale. The dedication on the part of the organization's young supporters to creating an environment conducive to lasting peace in even the most war-torn areas suggests that children all over the world believe that peace is possible, and are committed to realizing this dream through constructive action. Their achievements are a striking testament to the capacity of young people to engage in meaningful and effective actions in support of peace.

A Philosophy of Hope

Part of the philosophy of Free the Children is that we believe that the success of people of all ages in working towards peace both has been and must continue to be founded upon a philosophy of hope which encourages individuals from all walks of life to reach out beyond themselves in order to create a more just, tolerant and compassionate world. We have dubbed this approach to life one of "me to we", whereby people of all ages embrace service to others for the benefit of all. This approach is one that emphasizes the value of community and the importance of making common cause with the members of the local, national and global communities in which we all build our lives. While this philosophy certainly does have lofty goals, it is not one of distant dreams but rather of practical everyday life.

If our experiences with charitable work have taught us anything, it is that peace begins with the decisions that each of us make on a daily basis about how to interact with others and impact the world in which we live. In our lives we are all confronted with challenges both large and small. Everyday, we all have choices to make about how we will respond to the environment in which we find ourselves. In many ways this realization brings us back once again to the story of Christine, which began this contribution to this book, impressing upon us the power of ordinary people of all ages to hold hope and build peace through everyday decisions. Ultimately, peace is realized whenever we, like Christine, choose hope over despair, forgiveness over bitterness, compassion over cruelty and constructive action over inaction and destruction, and work to empower others to do the same.

PEACE IN THE 21ST CENTURY

Masami Saionji

As we look at today's world, we see continued warfare and strife, pollution, starvation, discrimination, persecution, and a host of other problems. In all parts of the world, people are living in fear of disease, environmental disaster, and the threat of violence and terrorism. Not only human beings, but animals, plants, the air, and all forms of life are suffering under a heavy burden of problems. What can we do to rise above these problems and create a better way of life in the twenty-first century?

In my view, the only way in which we can create a brighter future is for each and every one of us to make a clear change in our daily attitudes and ways of thinking. When each individual changes, the world will naturally change as a result.

All problems, whether big or small, come from within our individual selves. They do not come from others, nor do they arise outside us. Our individual problems, and the world's problems too, are caused by feelings hidden within each human heart—feelings like anger, resentment, intolerance toward others, vanity, greed, and competitiveness. Problems arise from our hunger to acquire more and more. Problems come from our boundless desire to increase our possessions and expand our power and authority. The world's problem is not race, religion, nationalism, discrimination, or persecution. Rather, it is ourselves. It is our very own consciousness.

At some point in time, we human beings lost our trust in the innate power, energy and wisdom that reside abundantly within us. Ever since that time, we have been judging ourselves and others, hating ourselves and others, and searching for solutions everywhere except within us.

Individual Responsibility

During the twentieth century, most individuals did not consider it their responsibility to put an end to the wars, poverty, hunger, and diseases that were spreading through the world. Rather, our minds were preoccupied with desires for our own personal happiness and prosperity.

Although it pained our hearts to hear of the tragic events going on in various regions, we, as individuals, felt that those tragedies were unrelated to ourselves. We took it for granted that the world's miseries should be resolved by governments and large-scale organizations such as the United Nations, UNICEF, the World Health Organization, the Red Cross, and various NGO's. We were convinced that we, as individuals, were not directly involved. We believed that the power of an individual was too small to make a difference. As a result of this way of thinking, each of us has turned away from our own responsibility. We have tried to shift our responsibility to something outside us.

But is this way of thinking correct? Do we, as individuals, really exist separately from our world? Does the responsibility for rescuing the world really reside outside us? My answer to this question is *No!*

As we progress through the 21st century, I believe that all human beings must develop an awareness of the part we each play in creating the world we live in. We are now stepping out of an age in which authority and responsibility were held by governments and various institutions—into an age when individual responsibility is paramount.

One by one, we must each come to see that individuals are not the subordinates of nations. Each individual is an embodiment of the same, one life of the universe, holding the same immense power to think, to choose, and to create. As soon as each individual develops a strong awareness of the limitless power and energy that we hold within us, and takes responsibility for his or her daily thoughts, words, and actions, I believe that all the sufferings of this world will naturally cease.

Do Not Imitate Our Mistakes

When I think of the young people who must guide this world to peace in the twenty-first century, from the bottom of my heart I wish to apologize. It was our responsibility to pass on to you a joyful world and a beautiful, peaceful environment. Instead, we have given you a world filled with fear and violence. How hard it must be for you to live in the world you inherited. Yet each of you holds a mission for changing the world, and you can surely do it if only you will trust yourselves.

There is just one thing I would like to ask of you. Please do not imitate our mistakes. Do not bow to others' opinions. Trust yourselves. Never doubt in yourselves on account of your age, or your background, or the extent of your experience. If you want to do something with your whole heart, try to do it and never give up.

In the twenty-first century, the important thing is not your nationality, or your culture, or how much money you have, or which school you attended. The important thing is *what you want to do*. Follow your own idea and your own intuition, and never be dissuaded by others.

Each of us has a unique role to play in creating peace during the twenty-first century. Recognizing the oneness of all life, let us respect and value our individual differences, and live with gratitude toward other people and everything in nature. Above all, we must believe in ourselves, and try to do what we really and truly wish to do. This, I believe, will light our way to peace in the twenty-first century.

PEACE AND SECURITY
Jonathan Granoff

We are the first generation making ethical decisions that will determine whether we will be the last generation. Science, technology and sophisticated social organizational skills have gifted us with unprecedented capacities for enrichment or destruction. I believe that there is an ethical responsibility to future generations to ensure we are not passing on a future of horrific wars or ecological catastrophe.

Our Collective Existence Is Fragile

Each of us knows that our individual life is precious and fragile. We are now reminded that our collective existence is fragile. This compels us to address, among other issues, ensuring bio-diversity and ending the destruction of thousands of species; reversing the depletion of fishing stocks; controlling ocean dumping; preventing ozone depletion; halting global warming; controlling and eliminating nuclear and other weapons of mass destruction; ending terrorism whether by States or non-State actors; fighting pandemic diseases; ending the tragedy of crushing poverty and lack of clean drinking water; and addressing crises arising from States in chaos. No nation or even a small group of nations can succeed in addressing these issues alone.

Some solutions must be universal. Chlorofluorocarbon from a refrigerant in the US or China can harm the ozone in Chile, New Zealand or anywhere. If one country allows oceanic dumping, others will follow. Viruses do not recognize religions, races or borders. Our futures are interconnected in unprecedented ways.

Wise people have been instructing us for millennia to recognize our deeper human unity. But, now necessity alerts us: the galvanizing power of moral leadership cannot be ignored in deference to short-term parochial interests. Our collective challenges require principles that are uplifting, inspiring, affirmative of our highest potential and universal. Hope must overcome fear.

Fear is the twin of ignorance, generating a false realism. Nicolo Machiavelli stated it in The Prince: "Where the safety of the country depends upon resolutions to be taken, no consideration of justice or injustice, humanity or cruelty, nor of glory or shame, should be allowed to prevail." This policy of "emergency" can hardly make sense as a norm if we are to be ethical beings living in community. Such so called "realists" invariably assert broadly that power in their own hands is necessary to ensure the security of their individual State.

Overlooking the intricate interconnectedness of living systems, they exalt social Darwinism. Strength is good, ultimate strength is better. In the quest for the ultimate weapon, an absurd result is obtained. The means to security and the pursuit of strength undermine the end of security. Such improved means to an unimproved end is most aptly articulated by nuclear weapons whereby the means of pursuing security undermines the end of security. This is not realistic. This is irresponsible.

These so called "realists" also rely on an inaccurate rigid world view in which the pursuit of the good and the pursuit of the real are divisible. They say that only what can be measured, predicted and controlled is relevant in policy discussion. What gives our lives meaning, what makes us human, what exalts our lives, is thus not considered. They leave little room in the making of policy for conscience, love, or other immeasurable, formless human treasures. Not the least of these treasures that give our lives meaning is compassion, the twin of wisdom.

Our Shared Golden Rules

Compassion is essential to our ethical nature and has universally guided every successful culture. It is upon the foundation of ethical principles that policies must become based. Without compassion, law cannot attain justice, and without justice, there is never peace. When kindness and compassion guide our policies, our rules become golden.

Buddhism: "Hurt not others in ways that you yourself would find hurtful." Udana-Varga, 5:18; "A state that is not pleasing or delightful to me, how could I inflict that upon another?" Samyutta Nikaya v. 353.

Christianity: "All things whatsoever you would that men should do to you, do you even so to them." Matthew 7:12.

Confucianism: "Do not unto others what you would not have them do unto you." Analects 15:23; "Tsi-kung asked, 'Is there one word that can serve as a principle of conduct for life?' Confucius replied, 'It is the word 'shu' — reciprocity. Do not impose on others what you yourself do not desire." Doctrine of the Mean 13.3; "One should not behave towards others in a way which is disagreeable to oneself." Mencius Vii.A.4.

Hinduism: "This is the sum of duty: do not unto others which would cause you pain if done to you." Mahabharata 5:1517.

Islam: "Not one of you is a believer until he desires for his brother that which he desires for himself." Hadith.

Jainism: "A man should journey treating all creatures as he himself would be treated." Sutrakritanga 1.11.33; "Therefore, neither does he [wise person] cause violence to others nor does he make others do so." Acarangasutra 5.101-2; "In happiness and suffering, in joy and grief, we should regard all creatures as we regard our own self." Lord Mahavira, 24th Tirthankara.

Judaism: ". . .thou shall love thy neighbor as thyself." Leviticus 19:18; "What is hateful to you, do not do to your fellow man. That is the law; all the rest is commentary." Talmud, Shabbat 31a.

Native American: "Respect for all life is the foundation." The Great Law of Peace.

Roman Pagan Religion: "The law imprinted on the hearts of all men is to love the members of society as themselves."

Shinto: "The heart of the person before you is a mirror." Sikhism: "I am a stranger to no one; and no one is a stranger to me. Indeed, I am a friend to all. Guru Granth Sahib, p. 1299. "As thou hast deemed thyself, so deem others."

Taoism: "Regard your neighbor's gain as your own gain, and your neighbor's loss as your own loss." Tai Shang Kan Ying Pien, 2 13-218.

Yoruba Wisdom (Nigeria): "One going to take a pointed stick to pinch a baby bird should first try it on himself to feel how it hurts."

Zoroastrianism: "That nature only is good when it shall not do unto another whatsoever is not good for its own self." Dadistan-I-Dinik, 94:5.

Philosopher's statements:

Plato: "May I do to others as I would that they should do unto me." Greece, 4th Century BCE.

Socrates: "Do not do to others that which would anger you if others did it to you." Greece, 5th Century BCE.

Seneca: "Treat your inferiors as you would be treated by your superiors." Epistle 47:11 Rome, 1st Century CE.

This principle of reciprocity is the ethical and moral foundation of all the world's major religions. Multilateralism is the logical political outgrowth of this principle. An international order based on cooperation, equity and the rule of law is its needed expression.

Where this rule of reciprocity is violated, instability follows. The failure of the nuclear weapons states to abide by their pledge, contained in the Nuclear Nonproliferation Treaty, to negotiate the elimination of nuclear weapons is the single greatest stimulus to the proliferation of nuclear weapons. For some to say nuclear weapons are good for them but not for others is simply not sustainable.

The threat to use nuclear weapons on innocent people can never be ethically legitimate. Thus, there is a moral imperative for their abolition.

Two New Rules

I would like to suggest two new rules:

The Rule of Nations: **"Treat other nations as you wish your nation to be treated."** The Rule of the Powerful: **"As one does, so shall others do."**

We are faced with a moment of collective truth: the ethical, spiritually-based insights of the wise coincide with material physical imperatives for survival. The value of the love of power must give way to the power of love. In today's world, leadership must be guided by the duty to love one's neighbor as oneself. This includes the duty to protect the weakest neighbor. And, today, the whole world is one neighborhood — a moral location, not just a physical one.

What was once an admonition as a personal necessity for inner growth has now become a principle that we must learn to utilize in forming public policies. The rule is offended by ethnic and religious exclusivity and prejudice, nationalistic expansionism, economic injustice and environmental irresponsibility.

How should we view the security of people? May I suggest that Timothy Wirth, when he was United States Under-Secretary of State for Global Affairs, was correct when he stated that a productive focus of multilateral security should begin with people: Security is now understood in the context of human security. Human security is about the one billion individuals who live in abject poverty. It is about the 800 million people who go hungry every day—the 240 million malnourished. The 17 million who die each year from easily preventable diseases fall into this definition of security, as do the 1.3 billion people without access to clean water and the more than 2 billion people who do not benefit from safe sanitation.

Failure to change from the flawed paradigm in which security is pursued primarily through violence reinforces the brutality inflicted upon millions of daily lives destroyed by conventional weapons, including small arms and anti-personnel land mines. And we cannot overlook the exorbitant economic waste and social costs of militarism—more than ten trillion dollars since the end of the Cold War. If we do not quickly get over the ridiculous excessive attachment to that which divides us, we will fail to establish effective institutions and policies in our time and we will fail to treat future generations as we would be treated. Such failure cannot be accepted by any parent who has looked into the eyes of their children.

A Technology to Melt the Human Heart

We have developed excessively sophisticated technologies for destruction. For our survival, we require appropriate social and human technologies for cooperation, for disarmament—for our very humanity.

An Eskimo elder at the Millennium World Peace Summit at the United Nations said, "Our history goes back 40,000 years and only now are we finding lakes in the Artic ice cap. You have technology that is melting the ice. When will we develop a technology to melt the human heart?"

THE RACE TO SAVE THE HUMAN RACE

Benjamin Ferencz

The historical record shows that international norms designed to maintain peace are gradually acquiring a mandatory character, but there is still a very long way to go. Sovereign states chose to ignore the 1955 warning by fifty-five Nobel Laureates that nations would cease to exist if they did not renounce the use of nuclear force. In 1994, my book *New Legal Foundations for Global Survival* warned, "It must be anticipated that the legal prohibitions against the use of armed might will be ignored by some well-armed or terroristic fanatics who are not prepared to be bound by the rules and who refuse to recognize the enormous perils of the nuclear age." The pace of change in traditional thinking has to be accelerated to meet the needs and expectations of a transformed world that is increasingly complicated and interdependent. The courts at Nuremberg held, and the UN confirmed, in 1946, that no nation and no person has the right to commit aggression, genocide or crimes against humanity against anyone. The ends, no matter how laudable, will never justify such means.

Global Problems Require Global Solutions

Today, global problems can only be resolved by global solutions. New institutions are needed to make the world function more efficiently and effectively. Until such agencies are created with global reach and vision that try to ameliorate justified complaints, violence will increase rather than diminish. The UN Charter must be interpreted in ways that enable the UN Organization to carry out its peaceful and social purposes. All that is suggested is that nations live up to their legal commitments. The Security Council has been vested with the authority to do whatever is required to maintain peace. That was the assignment delegated to them in 1945. The nations that sit on the Council have failed to discharge their most important duty. They never gave the Charter a chance. All States must honor the purpose and principles of the Charter in the spirit originally intended. Powerful world leaders cling to the status quo and lack the political will to make vital changes required to maintain peace. The world has become too dangerous to leave peace to the politicians. It is time for the voices of the people to be heard, loud and clear.

The issue facing future generations is whether human intelligence can overcome antiquated slogans and myths that threaten human survival. It should be obvious to all that the only victor in war is Death. Yet, war continues to be glorified. People everywhere share a common desire for peace and human dignity. Whether we help each other or kill each other depends on us. Many still believe that the only way to protect national interest is through the use of military power. They echo the 1881 sentiments of Prussian Field-Marshal von Moltke that war "is a link in God's world order." These are self-styled "Realists" who mock the "Idealists." After World War II, the victorious US Generals Dwight D. Eisenhower and Douglas MacArther, who would hardly be described as "Dreamers," were among countless other military leaders who joined in the denunciation of war as an instrument of national policy. The wise, and conservative, Professor Myres MacDougal of Yale recognized that today no people and no nation can be secure unless all are secure.

The hard-liners must be persuaded that their militant poli-cies are leading the world to ultimate destruction. The voices of the "Idealists" ~ must be loud enough to be heard by those "Realists" who now hold the reins of power in their hands. People must have the courage to stand and speak up for what they know is right. In the nuclear age, every rational mind must recognize that law is better than war. Moderation, compassion and compromise must find a home in the human heart.

Action

The first step in achieving any goal is to believe that it can be done. The next step is to make it happen! The frightened public will not remain indifferent forever to the broken prom-ises on which they depended for their security and tranquility. Television, film and the free worldwide Internet now offer educational tools that were unimaginable not long ago. Teach-ing institutions throughout the world are being mobilized to understand the requirements for a more humane and peace-ful universe. Religious congregations of all denominations recognize their common advantage in fostering tolerance and peaceful collaboration rather than conflict. Peace publications are proliferating and thousands of new non-governmental organizations are campaigning for peace-related goals. An enlightened public must make plain to the media and their advertisers that glorification of violence and killing is danger-ous to their public as well as their purse. Contrary to popular myth, war is bad for business; it destroys national economies and disrupts normal trade on which human welfare and well-being depend.

Every intelligent person must realize, as US President Ronald Reagan acknowledged, that nuclear weapons can never be used; they are homicidal, genocidal and suicidal. It should be possible to persuade those who support military budgets costing trillions of dollars that investing only a sliver of those sums to create new institutions, that may help prevent wars, is the best hope for avoiding atrocities and protecting the courageous young people who serve in the armed forces. The goals are attainable but it is up to the people themselves to create the conditions for a more secure future. The torchbearers who never fail to strive for peace shall be rewarded by the knowledge that they participated in the race to save the human race.

CREATING PEACE
Rodrigo Carazo Odio

The first phase of peace is tolerance and respect for all fellow beings, even those who have offended us. The true foundation of ideological pluralism has to be found through respect of others and their ideas. Education for peace must make humanity abandon the idea that culture, ideology, or ways of thinking can be imposed on others through violence or by force. The struggle for disarmament, therefore, must be accompanied by a pedagogy of peace. In other words, education for peace.

Disarmament may serve to avert imminent disaster. Education for peace is a permanent attitude. It has to last long generations. Disarmament means discarding an instrument of war in order to achieve the objective of peace. But educating for peace means creating the real and permanent conditions for a peaceful world. Consequently, disarmament should advance hand in hand with education for peace. Educating for peace should be a concrete practice, a concrete expression of a new vision of the triumphant dynamic peace, a new vision of peace as a result of consciousness.

Education for peace is not the study of peace, but the development of a discipline whose primary objective is to contribute—through research, teaching, dissemination and free inquiry—to the cause of peace.

For historical reasons, the prevailing concept of peace has been closer to the notion of peace as the absence of war, than the real concept, which is peace as the supreme achievement of humanity, as a continuing task in the domain of learning. Peace is a dynamic concept. It is a way of life. And consequently, one of the fundamental human rights. Viewing the matter in this way, it becomes a question not of keeping peace, but of achieving it.

Peace Is a Right and a Duty

Peace is a right of the human species, but it is also a duty. It follows that every human being and humankind as a whole, must be not only the object, but the subject of peace. Men and women may enjoy this right, but they have a duty at the same time of keeping it in being.

Today, however, nations prepare for war in order to achieve peace, but this is nothing other than to try to enforce the prevalence of fear and greed. Greed is one of the most active components of the destruction of peace. Peace is the work of justice and the fruit of love, but it must also be the product of education, or better said: education must be one of its most effective instruments of action.

Our national anthem in Costa Rica sings to our land and ends with a verse: "May work and peace live forever." When we work for peace, when we are teachers of peace, the benefits multiply. Peace is made through our work and we reap the benefits of peace from our work. To become a teacher of peace, we must open our hearts and let our feelings guide our minds. We must allow our intelligence to obey sentiments guided by love.

Peace Is a Way of Life

Peace is a way of life. It is the very pulse of life. Peace is not found; it is built. Peace is something that is achieved through sacrifice. If you want peace, work for peace. Peace begins within each one of us. It stems from the mind that obeys the heart that loves. Forgive those who have offended you and you will create peace. Let criticism pass without comment and you will make peace. Feel pain for the suffering of others and you will help create peace.

When, as President of the Republic of Costa Rica, I proposed a creation of a University for Peace, I tried to share the vivid feelings of the people of my country with the United Nations declaring peace to the world. Costa Rica is a country that never knew slavery as an independent country. It is a country where compulsory basic education was established in 1869, a country in which capital punishment was abolished in 1882. Costa Rica abolished its army as an institution in 1949. In 1983, the government declared our country a neutral and unarmed state, a move that contributed to the peace process in Central America. That is why I always repeat that I come from a peaceful country that has always tried to solve its problems through some form of dialogue inspired by reason.

Conflict will always exist among people. What we must learn is how to deal with that conflict without resorting to violence. When necessary, my country has defended itself against outside aggression. We had no other alternative. But as soon as the pain disappeared, we forgave and forgot.

At this beginning of the 21st century we are being called upon to face, in all its tragic urgency, the needs of humankind. However, we must at the same time, face up to the requirements of the species, for this 21st century shall be peaceful or shall not be at all.

100 IDEAS FOR CREATING A MORE PEACEFUL WORLD

David Krieger

Creating world peace takes many forms, but surely it begins with individuals. Here are 100 ideas for creating a more peaceful world. I encourage you to play your part in creating peace. It continues to be the most significant challenge of humankind, and requires the efforts of each of us.

1. Be generous with your smiles.
2. Be kind.
3. Respect the Earth.
4. Walk in a forest.
5. Plant a tree.
6. Contemplate a mountain.
7. Protect the Earth.
8. Live simply.
9. Help feed the hungry.
10. Erase a border in your mind.
11. Teach peace to children.
12. Read Chief Seattle's Letter to the President.
13. Be honest.
14. Demand honesty from your government.
15. Think about consequences.
16. Commit yourself to nonviolence.
17. Support nonviolent solutions to global problems.

18. Speak up for a healthy planet.
19. Demand reductions in military expenditures.
20. Be fair.
21. Pledge allegiance to the Earth and to its varied life forms.
22. Think for yourself.
23. Ask questions.
24. Recognize your unique potential.
25. Join an organization working for peace.
26. Be less materialistic.
27. Be more loving.
28. Empower others to work for peace.
29. Oppose all weapons of mass destruction.
30. Support equality.
31. Speak out for a nuclear weapons-free world.
32. Support a Department of Peace.
33. Listen to your heart.
34. Help the poor.
35. Fight against militarism.
36. Study the lives of peace heroes.
37. Help create a community peace park or garden.
38. Commemorate the International Day of Peace.
39. Help strengthen the United Nations.
40. Support the International Criminal Court.
41. Read the Universal Declaration of Human Rights.
42. Advance the rights of future generations.
43. Be a voice for the voiceless.
44. Join an action alert network.
45. Be forgiving.
46. Laugh more.
47. Play with a child.
48. Support education and the arts over weapons.
49. Help educate the next generation to be compassionate.

50. Take personal responsibility for creating a better world.
51. Sing.
52. Write a poem.
53. Organize a church service on the theme of peace.
54. Learn about another culture.
55. Help someone.
56. Support the UN Children's Fund (UNICEF).
57. Oppose the arms trade.
58. Clear your mind.
59. Breathe deeply.
60. Sip tea.
61. Express your views on peace to government officials.
62. Fight for the environment.
63. Celebrate Earth Day.
64. Think like an astronaut, recognizing that we have only one Earth.
65. Be constructive.
66. Let someone else go first.
67. Plant seeds of peace.
68. Work in a garden.
69. Change a potential enemy into a friend.
70. Be positive.
71. Share.
72. Be a good neighbor.
73. Send a note of appreciation.
74. Tell your friends how much they matter.
75. Say "I love you" more.
76. Don't tolerate prejudice.
77. Demand more from your elected officials.
78. Walk by the ocean, a river, or a lake.
79. Recognize that all humans have the right to peace.
80. Respect the dignity of each person.
81. Be a leader in the struggle for human decency.

82. Be a friend.
83. Send sunflowers to world leaders, and call for a world free of nuclear weapons.
84. Oppose technologies that harm the environment.
85. Lose an argument to a loved one.
86. Value diversity.
87. Walk softly on the Earth.
88. Appreciate the power of the sun.
89. Speak out for global disarmament.
90. Support a democratic order.
91. Teach non-violence by example.
92. Remember that "No man is an Island."
93. Spend time in nature.
94. Boycott war toys.
95. Be thankful for the miracle of life.
96. Seek harmony with nature.
97. Remind your leaders that peace matters.
98. Oppose violence in television programming for children.
99. Listen to Beethoven's Ode to Joy.
100. Celebrate peace.

REALIZING YOUR FULL POTENTIAL
David Krieger

Aspiring to reach one's full potential is a noble pursuit. But if military discipline and war are a society's benchmark to "be all you can be," then we need to rethink our values. More appropriate examples of lives to emulate are those of great peace leaders.

The most respected and revered peace leaders of modern times have helped keep hope alive by their indomitable spirits—Gandhi with his unrelenting non-violence and commitment to truth; Martin Luther King, Jr. with his passion for justice and dream of equal rights for all; Dorothy Day with her uncompromising commitment to peace and justice. We continue to be inspired by other great leaders—Rosa Parks with her profound assertion of human equality in refusing to sit in the back of the bus; Nelson Mandela with his endurance of the seemingly unendurable and his great human dignity; Archbishop Desmond Tutu with his embrace of humanity and the power of forgiveness; and the XIVth Dalai Lama with his unrelenting goodwill and simple, yet profound wisdom.

These leaders, and many more like them, put into daily action their beliefs that we can build a more decent, humane and just world. Their ambitions were shaped by a dedication to rising above the towering obstacles on the path to a better life for all because they understood that humanity is worth struggling for. Their dreams extended beyond the horizons of their times, and continue to give hope to people everywhere. They demonstrated their dedication by struggling for peace, justice and human decency through good times and bad. Above all, they exhibited courage, compassion and commitment.

Gandhi reflected the powerful sense of hope residing in all of these leaders, even in the darkest of times, when he said: "When I despair, I remember that all through history the way of truth and love has always won. There have been tyrants and murderers and for a time they seem invincible but in the end, they always fall—think of it, always."

The great peace leaders of our time were not born on Mount Olympus. They were and are ordinary mortals who distinguished themselves by their dedication to building a better world. Some lost their lives in their struggle, but they all walked unflinchingly on the path of truth and justice. They all cared more for their fellow humans than for riches. Those who are still alive, continue their relentless efforts on behalf of humanity. Their voices ring out for peace and call us to attention. Their actions stand as testaments to heroism, and beckon us to follow.

Each of us has the capacity for greatness in the cause of human decency. To make a difference we need only set our intentions and take the first step, which will lead to the second and the third. By our kindness, we will spread kindness. By our decency, we will spread decency. By our love, we will spread love. We all have the power to say No to war and Yes to peace. People do it every day. Some fifteen million people did it, taking to the streets in protest, prior to the initiation of the illegal invasion of Iraq in 2003. We don't always win, but with each act of peace we build hope, and with hope we are fortified to continue the struggle for peace.

We live on a miraculous planet, teeming with life and beauty, and it is our responsibility to preserve this wondrous place. It will take heart and courage and hope to defend the Earth, our source of life, but what could be more important? We will build friendships and community in our struggles. We will make our lives full and meaningful. We will stand in the shoes of those who struggled before us and help pave the way for those who will follow us. We fulfill our responsibilities as humans when we stand for peace and justice and are defenders of all life.

Here are some lessons I have tried to live by, and I pass them on to you. They have the power to enable each of us to realize our potential, to engage the best and most decent parts of our humanity, and to make us more powerful in our efforts to create a peaceful and just world.

1. Learn from others, but think for yourself. (Use your mind and judgment.)
2. Decide for yourself what is right or wrong. (Use your conscience.)
3. Speak out for what you believe in. (Use your voice.)
4. Stand up for what is right. (Use your power as an individual.)
5. Set goals and be persistent in working for them. (Use your vision and determination.)
6. Live by the Golden Rule. (Use your feelings as a point of reference.)
7. Recognize the miracle that you are. (Be spiritually aware.)
8. Never harm another miracle. (Be nonviolent.)
9. Believe in yourself. (Be trustworthy, even to yourself.)
10. Help others. (Be giving.)
11. Be a citizen of the world. (Be inclusive and embrace all life.)
12. Be a force for peace and justice. (Be courageous and committed.)

None of us, not even the greatest of peace leaders, can change the world alone, but we can commit ourselves to the great challenges of achieving a peaceful planet. We don't need to be passive in the face of wrongdoing nor live in the confines of narrow forms of nationalism. We don't need to remain ignorant and apathetic. We can make a difference. Our lives do matter. We have the power of choice. We can choose to hold hope and wage peace, and make ourselves worthy of our place on this extraordinary planet.

Declaration on the Right of Peoples to Peace Approved by General Assembly Resolution 39/11 November 12, 1984

The General Assembly,

Reaffirming that the principal aim of the United Nations is the maintenance of international peace and security,

Bearing in mind the fundamental principles of international law set forth in the Charter of the United Nations,

Expressing the will and the aspirations of all peoples to eradicate war from the life of mankind and, above all, to avert a world-wide nuclear catastrophe,

Convinced that life without war serves as the primary international prerequisite for the material well-being, development and progress of countries, and for the full implementation of the rights and fundamental human freedoms proclaimed by the United Nations,

Aware that in the nuclear age the establishment of a lasting peace on Earth represents the primary condition for the preservation of human civilization and the survival of mankind,

Recognizing that the maintenance of a peaceful life for peoples is the sacred duty of each State,

1. Solemnly proclaims that the peoples of our planet have a sacred right to peace;

2. Solemnly declares that the preservation of the right of peoples to peace and the promotion of its implementation constitute a fundamental obligation of each State;

3. Emphasizes that ensuring the exercise of the right of peoples to peace demands that the policies of States be directed

towards the elimination of the threat of war, particularly nuclear war, the renunciation of the use of force in international relations and the settlement of international disputes by peaceful means on the basis of the Charter of the United Nations;

4. Appeals to all States and international organizations to do their utmost to assist in implementing the right of peoples to peace through the adoption of appropriate measures at both the national and the international level.

A UNITED WORLD OR A DIVIDED WORLD? MULTIETHNICITY, HUMAN RIGHTS, TERRORISM

World Summit of Nobel Peace Laureates
November 12, 2004, Rome, Italy

Final Statement of the 5th Summit of Nobel Peace Laureates

Two decades ago, the world was swept with a wave of hope. Inspired by the popular movements for peace, freedom, democracy and solidarity, the nations of the world worked together to end the cold war. Yet the opportunities opened up by that historic change are slipping away. We are gravely concerned with the resurgent nuclear and conventional arms race, disrespect for international law and the failure of the world's governments to address adequately the challenges of poverty and environmental degradation. A cult of violence is spreading globally; the opportunity to build a culture of peace, advocated by the United Nations, Pope John Paul II, the Dalai Lama and other spiritual leaders, is receding.

Alongside the challenges inherited from the past there are new ones, which, if not properly addressed, could cause a clash of civilizations, religions and cultures. We reject the idea of the inevitability of such a conflict. We are convinced that combating terrorism in all its forms is a task that should be pursued with determination. Only by reaffirming our shared ethical values—respect for human rights and fundamental freedoms—and by observing democratic principles, within and amongst countries, can terrorism be defeated. We must address the root causes of terrorism—poverty, ignorance and injustice—rather than responding to violence with violence.

Unacceptable violence is occurring daily against women and children. Children remain our most important neglected treasure. Their protection, security and health should be the highest priority. Children everywhere deserve to be educated in and for peace. There is no excuse for neglecting their safety and welfare and, particularly, for their suffering in war.

The war in Iraq has created a hotbed of dangerous instability and a breeding ground for terrorism. Credible reports of the disappearance of nuclear materials cannot be ignored. While we mourn the deaths of tens of thousands of people, none of the goals proclaimed by the coalition have been achieved.

The challenges of security, poverty and environmental crisis can only be met successfully through multilateral efforts based on the rule of law. All nations must strictly fulfill their treaty obligations and reaffirm the indispensable role of the United Nations and the primary responsibility of the UN Security Council for maintaining peace.

We support a speedy, peaceful resolution of the North Korean nuclear issue, including a verifiable end to North Korea's nuclear weapons program, security guarantees and lifting of sanctions on North Korea . Both the six-party talks and bilateral efforts by the United States and North Korea should contribute to such an outcome.

We welcome recent progress in the talks between Iran and Great Britain, France and Germany on the Iranian nuclear program issue and hope that the United States will join in the process to find a solution within the framework of the International Atomic Energy Agency.

We call for the reduction of military expenditures and for conclusion of a treaty that would control arms trade and prohibit sales of arms where they could be used to violate international human rights standards and humanitarian law.

As Nobel Laureates, we believe that the world community needs urgently to address the challenges of poverty and sustainable development. Responding to these challenges requires the political will that has been so sadly lacking.

The undertakings pledged by states at the UN Millennium Summit, the promises of increased development assistance, fair trade, market access and debt relief for developing countries, have not been implemented. Poverty continues to be the world's most widespread and dangerous scourge. Millions of people become victims of hunger and disease, and entire nations suffer from feelings of frustration and despair. This creates fertile ground for extremism and terrorism. The stability and future of the entire human community are thus jeopardized.

Scientists are warning us that failure to solve the problems of water, energy and climate change will lead to a breakdown of order, more military conflicts and ultimately the destruction of the living systems upon which civilization depends. Therefore, we reaffirm our support for the Kyoto Protocol and the Earth Charter and endorse the rights-based approach to water, as reflected in the initiative of Green Cross International calling upon governments to negotiate a framework treaty on water.

As Nobel Peace Prize Laureates we believe that to benefit from humankind's new, unprecedented opportunities and to counter the dangers confronting us there is a need for better global governance. Therefore, we support strengthening and reforming the United Nations and its institutions.

As immediate specific tasks, we commit to work for:

- Genuine efforts to resolve the Middle East crisis. This is both a key to the problem of terrorism and a chance to avoid a dangerous clash of civilizations. A solution is possible if the right of all nations in the region to secure, viable statehood is respected and if the Middle East is integrated in all global processes while respecting the unique culture of the peoples of that region.

- Preserving and strengthening the Nuclear Non-Proliferation Treaty. We reject double standards and emphasize the legal responsibility of nuclear weapons states to work to eliminate nuclear weapons. We call for continuation of the moratorium on nuclear testing pending entry into force of the Comprehensive Test Ban Treaty, and for accelerating the process of verifiable and irreversible nuclear arms reduction. We are gravely alarmed by the creation of new, usable nuclear weapons and call for rejection of doctrines that view nuclear weapons as legitimate means of war-fighting and threat pre-emption.

- Effectively realizing the initiative of the UN Secretary General to convene a high-level conference in 2005 to give an impetus to the implementation of the Millennium Development Goals. We pledge to work to create an atmosphere of public accountability to help accomplish these vitally important tasks.

We believe that to solve the problems that challenge the world today politicians need to interact with an empowered civil society and strong mass movements. This is the way toward a globalization with a human face and a new international order that rejects brute force, respects ethnic, cultural and political diversity and affirms justice, compassion and human solidarity.

We, the Nobel Peace Laureates and Laureate organizations, pledge to work for the realization of these goals and are calling on governments and people everywhere to join us.

– Mikhail Gorbachev, Kim Dae-Jung, Lech Walesa, Joseph Rotblat, Jose Ramos-Horta, Betty Williams, Mairead Corrigan Maguire, Carlos Filipe Ximenes Belo, Adolfo Perez Esquivel, and Rigoaberta Menchu Tum; and, United Nations Children's Fund, Pugwash Conferences, International Physicians for the Prevention of Nuclear War, International Peace Bureau, Institut de Droit International, American Friends Service Committee, Médicins sans Frontières, Amnesty International, United Nations High Commissioner for Refugees, International Labour Organization, International Campaign to Ban Land Mines, United Nations.

APPENDIX C

MAKE THE UNITED NATIONS EFFECTIVE FOR THE 21ST CENTURY*

Benjamin Ferencz and Ken Keyes, Jr.

Since the end of World War II, our failure to create an effective world system to govern the planet has resulted in millions killed, many more injured, businesses disrupted, lives twisted through fear and hatred, property destroyed, environmental pollution and degeneration accelerated, and money wasted on killing machines (this term includes both people and guns). The insanity of nuclear killing machines is making us realize that World War III (with possibly 5 *billion* fatalities) may bring about the end of all people on this planet. It is the plea of *PlanetHood* that we end the arms race—not the human race.

The First Four Steps

Let's briefly review the steps we've covered so far. Step One requires us to assert our ultimate human right to live with dignity in a healthy environment free from the threat of war. Step Two asks us to understand the new top layer of government we need in order to nail down this ultimate human right for you and your family for all time—no more international

* Benjamin Ferencz and Ken Keyes, Jr., Chapter 5, *Planethood* (Coos Bay, OR: Love Line Books 1991) 86-111.

anarchy. We need to complete the governmental structure of the world with a limiting constitution setting up a *lawmaking body* (representing the people of the world), a *world court* (staffed with the wisest judges chosen from among the nations of the world), and *an effective system of sanctions and peacekeeping forces* to enforce the agreed standards of national behavior. This final layer of government would globally ensure our basic human rights, protect the sovereignty of nations, settle disputes legally, and protect the environment.

By taking Step Three we realize what it means to become a Planethood Patriot. We are urged to step into George Washington's footsteps in creating and supporting a new constitution to govern the nations of the world. The Federal Republic of the World must be strong enough to avoid ineffectiveness, and have checks and balances to limit power and avoid tyranny. This is secured by a *wise balance of power* between the legislative, executive, and judicial branches.

In Step Four we acknowledge our enormous progress over the past century in creating international law. We have been gradually globalizing. We note how the nations of the world have been getting accustomed to working with each other—gradually *and safely* yielding small portions of their sovereignty in order to benefit from binding international agreements for the common good. We see that nation-states are already merging into larger economic and political entities to meet their common needs—such as the European Union. *There is a growing awareness that the world system must change to meet the challenge of the 21st Century.*

In Step Five we will discuss updating our vehicle for survival—the U.N.—as we move toward an effective world system with checks and balances to protect our rights and freedoms. This step is primarily concerned with spelling out how we need to reform the U.N. to ensure world peace.

After the carnage of World War II with 35 million dead,

many nations were determined not to go through that again. Toward the end of the war we began to plan the United Nations Organization. In October 1945 the Charter was ratified by 50 nations at San Francisco. Enthusiasm ran high. "The U.N. Charter can be a greater Magna Carta," said John Foster Dulles, our Secretary of State, who was a delegate to the San Francisco conference.

It's interesting to note that the U.N. Charter was completed on June 26, 1945—six weeks before Hiroshima and Nagasaki. This may help explain its weakness. The delegates were unaware of the devastation we would face in the nuclear era. They did not know that humanity's survival would be at stake. They failed to understand that we could no longer drag our feet in replacing international anarchy with enforced international law.

The Security Council

The Charter provides for a Security Council and a General Assembly. The Security Council was supposed to be the enforcement arm. Its five permanent members were victorious in World War II: the United States, the Soviet Union, Britain, France, and China (in 1971 the People's Republic of China replaced Nationalist China on the Security Council; in 1991, the Soviet Union was replaced by Russia). In addition, there are now ten rotating members—originally there were six.

It was deliberately set up so that the big powers could ignore any vote they didn't like. *Any one of the five permanent members of the Security Council can veto any enforcement action—even if the rest of the world is for it!* Since the Big Five have been behind most of the trouble in the world, it's like setting up the foxes to guard the chicken coop.

Because of the distrust and conflict between the Soviet Union and the United States (and because we usually vote to support our friends and they usually support their friends), deadlocks on all important issues involving war and peace have usually blocked effective action by the U.N. For example, the U.S. in 1990 vetoed a resolution for the U.N. to send a fact-finding mission to get information on the Jewish-Arab conflict in the occupied territories. An impartial understanding of what's happening is a needed first step in the peace process. This lack of respect for legal, peaceful conflict resolution has set a poor example for the other nations of the world.

Brian Urquhart, U.N. under secretary-general for special political affairs, lamented, "There are moments when I feel that only an invasion from outer space will reintroduce into the Security Council that unanimity and spirit which the founders of the Charter were talking about."

Thus we have a toddling Security Council that under the Charter is empowered to send armed forces anywhere on earth to stop war. And it is usually rendered impotent because of the Charter requirement for the unanimous vote of the permanent members of the Security Council to act in preserving peace. In 1945 we weren't quite ready yet to take the final step. Perhaps we're now waking up to the idiocy of living in an ungoverned world!

The General Assembly

In addition to the Security Council, the Charter of the United Nations set up the General Assembly. It has been called a "town meeting of the world" by former Secretary-General Trygve Lie. Each nation has one vote in the General Assembly, which has grown from the original 50 nations to 160 today. Thus, small nations, *regardless of size*, have the same vote as large nations, *regardless of population*. For example, Grenada with about 90,000 people has an equal vote with the United States, which has 1/4 billion people.

Since the Security Council has all the power to act, the big powers gave the other nations of the world the power to talk! Consequently, when a resolution passes the General Assembly, it goes to the Security Council *as a recommendation only*. The General Assembly has no Charter power to require any action to keep the peace—or to do anything but suggest!

Thus, we are heading for the 21st Century with 160 loose cannons in the world. "But the hard fact remains," comments Richard Hudson in his newsletter *Global Report*, "that the decision-making system in the world body is too flawed to deal with the awesome gamut of our planet's problems in the coming decades. It is neither morally right nor politically sensible to leave veto power in the Security Council in the hands of the five nuclear powers. It is plainly absurd to have decisions made on the basis of one nation, one vote in the General Assembly, thus giving countries with minute populations and minuscule contributions to the U.N. budget the same influence in decision-making as the bigger countries that have to pay the bills. Moreover, a central global decision-making body that can pass only non-binding recommendations is not what the world needs for the 21st century."

The Need for Reform

Patricia Mische, co-founder of Global Education Associates, tells a story that compares the United Nations to a dog that is expected to give protection from thieves and murderers. The dog is a good dog, but it has three problems. First, the masters muzzle the dog so the dog can bark but not bite, and thieves and murderers know this. Second, the masters don't feed the dog very well, so the dog is always hungry and anxious for itself, and lacks energy to do its job well. Third, the dog has 160 masters, and they often give conflicting directions and confuse the dog.

Here is the prescription for rebuilding the UN: Remove the muzzle, feed the dog, and reform the masters, so they will not be confusing the dog.

Vernon Nash wrote in *The World Must Be Governed*, ". . . if Hamilton or any other founding father returned to the United States today and read a. current article about the performance and prospects of the United Nations, he certainly would say to himself, 'This is where I came in.'. . . Then, as now, men kept trying to get order without law, to establish peace while retaining the right and power to go on doing as they pleased."

The United States, which was the principal mover in creating the World Court, gave the appearance of accepting compulsory jurisdiction over "any question of international law." But that was quite deceptive. By special reservations, the U.S. excluded certain types of disputes, which the U.S. could *by itself* decide it wanted solely within its own domestic jurisdiction.

A nation undermines the Court when it gives the appearance of accepting the Court and, at the same time, denies to the tribunal the normal powers of every judicial agency. *A nation that defies the Jurisdiction of the Court when it becomes a defendant shows contempt for the Court.* A nation that ignores the Court when it doesn't like a judgment against it undercuts the process of law. When these things are done by the U.S., which helped establish the World Court, it diminishes respect for itself.

Despite technical legal arguments that were raised to justify the U.S. position when Nicaragua in 1984 complained that we were mining its harbors and seeking to overthrow its government, the fact is that the U.S. refused to honor the Court or its judgments. This was seen throughout the world as a hypocritical manifestation of scorn for the tribunal—which the United States praised when decisions went in its favor. *Defiance of law is an invitation to disaster. What may have been tolerable in the prenuclear age is intolerable now.*

In a world of law and order, aggressor nations should clearly be identified as outlaws for rejecting the rule of law. This is not to suggest that justified grievances should be ignored; sincere efforts must be made to find just solutions. *But a handful of states, or a small group of fanatics, should not be permitted to thwart humankind's progress toward a more lawful and peaceful world.*

Supporting the U.N.

In 1986 the U.S. Congress reduced its financial support of the United Nations by over half, largely because it did not like certain expenditures. Since the total U.N. budget is less than New York City's, any reduction of its annual $800 million income is crippling. In the past, the Soviet Union has also failed to pay its U.N. dues for the same reason. In October 1987, Mikhail Gorbachev talked of invigorating the Security Council. To back up his words, the Soviet Union announced that it would pay all its overdue U.N. bills, which came to $197 million. And they followed through on this promise.

That left the United States in October 1987 the outstanding delinquent, who still owed over $414 million, including $61 million for peacekeeping forces that the U.S. opposed! As of December 1989, the U.S. was behind $518 million–in violation of its treaty obligations. In his last budget request, President Reagan asked for full U.N. current funding and about a 10% payment on our past dues. Bush in his first budget made the same request. Our Congress was still unwilling to honor our obligations. The cost of only one Stealth bomber would cover our disgracefully broken contractual agreements with the U.N.–and with humanity's future.

The world spends only $800 MILLION a year on peace through the U.N., and about $1 TRILLION on national military budgets–**over a thousand times more!!!** Does it come as a surprise that we are today 1,000 times more effective at waging war than at waging peace?

There are amazing parallels between our situation with the United Nations today and the dangerous situation in the United States two centuries ago. Tom Hudgens in his book *Let's Abolish War* points out that the Continental Congress under the Articles of Confederation:

1. Had no independent taxing powers.
2. Could not regulate interstate and foreign commerce.
3. Had no powers of direct enforcement of its laws.
4. Was ineffective in foreign affairs.
5. Had no chief executive.
6. Had no binding court of justice...

"Do you realize," Hudgens asks, "that every one of these charges can be leveled at the United Nations today? We are living today under the Articles of Confederation except we call it the United Nations."

Instead of starting all over again, the U.N. may be our best bet to rapidly ensure our ultimate human right. A redrafting of the Charter and its ratification by the nations of the world is needed. It won't be easy to persuade nations to mend their ways, but it can be done.

For years, the officials of the U.N. have known what needs to be done. They're powerless unless authorized by the nations of the world. They've been waiting for you to take the needed steps to alter the views of the entrenched diplomats, which would permit them to respond effectively to international lawlessness—and thus set the stage for a new era of prosperity and peace on earth.

Confederation vs. Federation

In order to take Step Five by working to make the U.N. more effective in the nuclear age, you must clearly understand the key differences between the U.N. today and the world federation we need for tomorrow. Just as the terms "Confederation" and

"Federation" were confusing to the 1787 delegates at Phila-
delphia, people usually don't understand their significance
today. The World Federalist Association in its pamphlet *We the
People* helps us clarify the crucial differences between a league
or confederation, and a federation or union:

- In a league or confederation (like the U.N.), each state
  does as it pleases regardless of the consequences to the
  whole; in a *federation* or *union* (like the U.S.), each state
  accepts some restrictions for the security and wellbeing
  of the whole.

- In a league, the central body is merely a debating society without authority to control the harmful behavior
  of individuals; in a *federation*, the central body makes
  laws for the protection of the whole and prosecutes
  individuals who break them.

- In a league, any enforcement is attempted only against
  member states; in a *federation*, enforcement of laws is
  directed against *individual* lawbreakers.

- In a league, conflicts among members continue un-
  abated, resulting in costly arms races and wars; in a
  federation, conflicts among states are worked out in a
  federal parliament and in federal courts.

- A league has no independent sources of revenue; a *federation* has its own supplemental sources of revenue.

- In a league, state loyalty overrides loyalty to the wider
  community; in a *federation*, loyalty to each state is bal-
  anced by loyalty to the wider community.

Finding the Best Way

Could you feel secure if a congress made up of people from all over the world enacted binding international laws? Would you be taken advantage of? Too heavily taxed? Your rights ignored? Could a dictator grab power? Can we set up a world legislature, court, and executive branch that will be more protective of the U.S. than the Pentagon? How can we actually increase our "defense" through a reformed U.N.? How do we reform the U.N. to avoid ecocide?

As George Washington and Benjamin Franklin would testify, there is no one simple way to hammer out a new constitution. It takes an open-minded willingness to consider all points of view, to lay aside one's prejudices and psychological certainties, and to be patient enough to listen and search until effective answers are found and agreed upon. Just as success in 1787 required that various states be satisfied, in like manner we must create a reformed U.N. that meets today's needs and interests of the nations of the world.

There have been many proposals to improve the United Nations and make it more effective as the keeper of the peace. One suggestion, known as the "Binding Triad," comes from Richard Hudson, founder of the Center for War/Peace Studies. It requires two basic modifications of the U.N. Charter:

> The voting system in the General Assembly would be changed. Important decisions would still be adopted with a single vote, *but with three simultaneous majorities within that vote.* Approval of a resolution would require that the majority vote include two-thirds of the members present and voting (as at present), nations representing two-thirds of the population of those present and voting, and nations representing two-thirds of the contributions to the regular U.N. budget of those present and voting. Thus, in order for a resolution to pass, it would have to be supported strongly by most of the countries of the world, most of the population of the world, and most of the political/economic/military strength of the world.

The powers of the General Assembly would be increased under the Binding Triad so that in most cases its resolutions would be binding, not recommendations as at present. The new General Assembly, now a global legislature, will be able to use peacekeeping forces and/or economic sanctions to carry out its decisions. However, the Assembly would not be permitted "to intervene in matters which are essentially within the jurisdiction of any state." If the jurisdiction were in doubt, the issue would be referred to the World Court, and if the court ruled that the question was essentially domestic, the Assembly could not act.

This is only one possibility for giving the General Assembly limited legislative powers. A World Constitution for the Federation of Earth has been drafted by the World Constitution and Parliament Association headed by Philip Isely of Lakewood, Colorado. There are many ways to reform the U.N. to give the world binding international laws, a binding court of international justice, and an executive branch to enforce the law with effective economic sanctions and an international military force *that replaces national armies, navies, and air forces.*

A 14-point program is shown on the next page. Models of new international systems to create world order have been prepared by many scholars, among who are Professor Richard Falk of Princeton University, Professor Saul Mendlovitz of Rutgers, and Professor Louis Sohn of Harvard University. With wise checks and balances, we can set up an overall system that will enable the world to work! Political leaders lack the political will to make the required changes in the U.N. It's time for the public to speak out.

Once the world union is formed, do we want to permit an easy divorce if a nation wants to get out when it disagrees about something? The American Civil War in 1861-1865 settled whether states could leave the federal union if they disagreed with its policies. The victory by the Union dearly established that no state could secede from the federal government once it agreed to be a member.

If politicians in a nation become angry and could whip up the people to get out, it would signal the end of the world system. Once a nation agrees to the reformed U.N., it must be permanent. "By resigning from the organization," Cord Meyer warns, "a nation could free itself from international supervision, forcing a renewal of the armament race and certain war. In view of the nature of the new weapons, secession would be synonymous with aggression."

As we've pointed out, *there is no one way* to transform the United Nations into an effective world government. It is important that you give thought to this vital matter and arrive at your own conclusions on how to do it. Then discuss them with your friends and neighbors, who will no doubt develop their own ideas. It is only from the clash of opinions that a living truth will emerge that will point to an effective way to complete the governmental structure of the world.

The Challenge of Our Age

We are at a crucial point in history. We are on the threshold of great progress. We have reached the stage where large-scale wars are no longer compatible with the future of the human race. We have gone beyond the point where such military power is protective. Instead it threatens to kill us all. We are gradually fouling our environment so that it cannot support human life. And we now know that we must have global institutions to solve our global problems.

"Environmental knowledge and concerns," according to Pamela Leonard, "have risen at an increasingly rapid rate in recent years, and many nations have enacted laws and set up agencies to deal with them. Yet little has been done to create laws or institutions on an international scale, despite the fact that the impacts of air and water pollutants travel as easily across national boundaries as across municipal boundaries."

Increasing Abundance

Even if we were not threatened by nuclear war or environmental ruin, we would benefit enormously by a reformed U.N. Through a world republic, our children will have greater prosperity, more personal opportunities for a good life, better maintenance of our precious planet, and better protection of their human rights and freedoms.

Imagine what a difference this would make in your life and that of your loved ones. The heavy taxes that spill your "economic blood" year by year would no longer be used to feed a greedy war machine. Your children could then feel confident that they would have a future. Business could be liberated from the import and export fences that limit opportunities. We could effectively begin to improve the quality of the air we breathe and the water we drink. Education, medical care, and quality of life would vastly improve when the world no longer spent $1.5 million each minute on increasing its killing capacity. *A small international peacekeeping force of several hundred thousand well-trained and equipped people could replace the millions of soldiers now under arms who constantly disrupt the peace of the planet.*

Over the past several centuries there has been a gradual awakening to the importance of international law that can override the military passions of the 160 separate nations around the globe. We have tried world courts and have found that they work if we want them to. We have set up international organizations such as the League of Nations and the United Nations. Each has been a step forward. All this experimenting, testing, trying, and hoping *have been important steps up the ladder of international growth* toward the completion of the governance of our world. We now have the glorious challenge of creating lasting peace and prosperity by reforming the United Nations into a world republic.

Approaching Planethood

Many nations today, and eventually all nations, will be willing to cooperate in a reformed United Nations. They will respond to the insistence of their people that we do not let our planet be ruined or blown apart through war. These nations will want to benefit from the much safer and far less costly protection of their national rights and freedoms that *only a world government can offer them.*

At long last, the people of this world would be able to get out of the arms race and enjoy a much higher standard of living, environmental protection, education, culture, medical care, etc. We need a world governance that, unlike the present Security Council, cannot be vetoed by one of the five victorious nations of World War II. It will be able to effectively respond to environmental problems that threaten the security of everyone everywhere.

It is now time for the people to insist on reforming the U.N. Charter. They will become a powerful force when they *unite and act together.* Sooner or later, those who resist at first will join in—just as holdout states discovered *they could not afford to pass up the many benefits* of becoming a part of the United States two centuries ago.

The draft of the U.N. Charter was discussed at Dumbarton Oaks, a private estate in Washington, DC. On a tablet in the garden was inscribed a prophetic motto: "As ye sow, so shall ye reap." When the final instrument was accepted by 50 nations on June 26, 1945, everyone knew that it was less than perfect. The Secretary of State reported to President Truman: "What has resulted is a human document with human imperfections but with human hopes and human victory as well."

We need a new "Dumbarton Oaks" to the 21st Century. On December 23, 1987, our Congress passed a law calling for the appointment by our President of a bipartisan U.S. Commission to Improve the Effectiveness of the United Nations. Commissioners should have been appointed by June 1, 1989. By August 1990 there was still no indication that our President would comply with this law of Congress. Let the voice of the people be heard!

Send a copy of *PlanetHood* to the President and to your congressional leaders. Tell them you're tired of delay and indecision. If they get flooded with reminders from the voters, they'll soon take notice. It is time to act NOW so that the dreams of the U.N. founders may finally become a reality

We can no longer pretend that we don't know what needs to be done. How long will it be until a president, prime minister, or general secretary calls for a Conference to Reform the United Nations or an International Constitutional Convention—and invites all nations to send delegates? Here is an opportunity for statesmanship and fame of the highest order. Let us seize this history-making opportunity and accept the challenge to create a more peaceful world.

Like Paul Revere, let's awaken our neighbors. Let's give ourselves effective international law, world courts, and enforcement in a safe system of checks and balances. Let's work continuously to bring about the day when our front lines of defense consist of brigades of international attorneys practicing before a binding world court. Then we'll have finally secured our ultimate human right to live in dignity in a healthy environment free from the threat of war.

We need a reliable cop on the international corner. Will you help our ungoverned world to create a world system that can work?

You'll be taking the Fifth Step toward planethood when you play your part in making the U.N. effective for the 21st Century. As a Planethood Patriot, you'll know that you are doing what you can to make your life count. You will have saved yourself, your family, and all of the men, women, and children throughout our beautiful planet—now and for generations to come.

IT DEPENDS ON YOU!

A 14-POINT PROGRAM for Reforming the United Nations

1. Improve the General assembly decision-making process.
2. Modify the veto in the Security Council.
3. Create an International Disarmament Organization.
4. Improve the dispute settlement process.
5. Improve the U.N.'s peacekeeping capability.
6. Provide for adequate and stable U.N. revenues.
7. Create an International Court of Justice.
8. Create an International Criminal Court to try hijackers and terrorists.
9. Improve the U.N.'s human rights machinery.
10. Create stronger U.N. environmental and conservation programs.
11. Provide international authorities for areas not under national control.
12. Provide for more effective world trade and monetary systems.
13. Establish a U.N. development program.
14. Achieve administrative reform of the U.N. system.

ABOUT THE AUTHORS

Walter Cronkite was the only journalist to be voted among the top ten "most influential decision-makers in America" and was also named the "most influential person" in broadcasting in surveys conducted by US News and World Report. In his more than 65 years of journalism, he has covered virtually every major news event of the twentieth century. He began as a United Press (UP) correspondent in WWII and covered the Nuremberg Trials. He served as UP Bureau Chief in Moscow from 1946-48. In 1950 he joined CBS in Washington, D.C. and moved to New York in 1954 where he pioneered the first evening news broadcast as Anchorman, and later Managing Editor, for the CBS Evening News. For the next three decades he covered such history-making events as the U.S. Space Program; the assassinations of President John F. Kennedy, Dr. Martin Luther King, Jr. and Senator Robert Kennedy; and the Watergate scandal and the Vietnam War, to name a few. He interviewed every U.S. President since FDR and the major Heads of State before stepping down from his Anchor desk in 1981 to assume his current role as Special Correspondent for CBS News. In a nationwide viewer opinion survey conducted as recently as 1995, more than a decade after leaving the CBS anchor desk, he again was voted "Most Trusted Man in Television News."

He is the author of six books, including his autobiography, A *Reporter's Life*; hosts and narrates numerous documentaries for PBS and the Discovery Channel; maintains an active international lecture schedule; and most recently wrote a nationally syndicated newspaper column for more than 175 newspapers around the country. In 2004, he received the Nuclear Age Peace Foundation's Distinguished Peace Leadership Award.

Adam Curle, Ph.D., is an English Quaker and peacemaker. He has worked around the world, helping people find just and peaceful resolutions to a broad array of conflicts, from familial to international. Reflecting on his wealth of experience, he developed a model for proper sequencing of conflict-resolution and nonviolent-action processes. Among his academic accomplishments, Curle was a consultant on education policy in Pakistan from 1956-1964 and served as a Professor of Education at the University of Ghana in 1959. In 1962, Curle set up Harvard Center for Studies in Education and Development and was chosen as the first professor of Peace Studies at the University of Bradford in 1973. He is author of many books, including *To Tame The Hydra: Undermining The Culture Of Violence* (2000). For more information, visit the University of Bradford's *Peace Times* online at www.brad.ac.uk/acad/peace/ptimes/peacetimes.htm

Benjamin B. Ferencz, J.D. was a Prosecutor at the Nuremberg War Crimes Trials. After he graduated from Harvard Law School in 1943, he joined an anti-aircraft artillery battalion preparing for the invasion of France. As an enlisted man under General Patton, he fought in every campaign in Europe. As Nazi atrocities were uncovered, he was transferred to a newly created War Crimes Branch of the Army to gather evidence of Nazi brutality and apprehend the criminals. On the day after Christmas 1945, Ferencz was honorably discharged from the US Army with the rank of Sergeant of Infantry. He returned to New York and prepared to practice law. Shortly thereafter, he was recruited as a Prosecutor for the Nuremberg war crimes trials. Twenty-two defendants were charged with murdering over a million people. He was only twenty-seven years old. It was his first case. All of the defendants were convicted. Thirteen were sentenced to death. The verdict was hailed as a great success for the prosecution. Ferencz's primary objective had been to establish a legal precedent that would encourage a more humane and secure world in the future.

In addition to uncounted articles on international law and peace, Ferencz is the author of a number of books including, *Defining International Aggression-The Search for World Peace*; *An International Criminal Court-A Step Toward World Peace*; *Enforcing International Law: A Way to World Peace*; *A Common Sense Guide to World Peace*; and *PlanetHood* with Ken Keyes, Jr. Ferencz was also instrumental in establishing the International Criminal Court (ICC). He is Adjunct Professor of International Law at Pace University and founder of the Pace Peace Center. He continues to write and speak worldwide for international law and global peace. For more information, visit Ben Ferencz' official website at www.benferencz.org.

Jane Goodall, Ph.D., is a renowned primatologist. In 1965, she earned her doctorate in Ethology from Cambridge University. Dr. Goodall's scores of honors include the Medal of Tanzania, the National Geographic Society's Hubbard Medal, Japan's prestigious Kyoto Prize, the Prince of Asturias Award for Technical and Scientific Research 2003, the Benjamin Franklin Medal in Life Science, and the Gandhi/King Award for Nonviolence. In April 2002 Secretary-General Annan named Dr. Goodall a United Nations "Messenger of Peace." In 2003, Queen Elizabeth II named Dr. Goodall a Dame of the British Empire. Dr. Goodall has received honorary doctorates from numerous universities. Dr. Goodall's list of publications is extensive, including two overviews of her work at Gombe, as well as two autobiographies in letters and a spiritual autobiography, *Reason for Hope*. Her many children's books include *Grub: the Bush Baby*, *Chimpanzees I Love: Saving Their World and Ours* and *My Life with the Chimpanzees*. *The Chimpanzees of Gombe: Patterns of Behavior* is recognized as the definitive work on chimpanzees and is the culmination of Jane Goodall's scientific career. She has been the subject of numerous television documentaries and is featured in the large-screen format film, *Jane Goodall's Wild Chimpanzees* (2002). For more information, please visit The Goodall Institute at www.janegoodall.org.

Jonathan Granoff, Esq., has for more than 20 years contributed his legal expertise, developed as a successful private attorney, to the movement to eliminate nuclear weapons. Mr. Granoff was elected President of the Global Security Institute after the death of the Institute's founding president, Senator Alan Cranston (1914-2000). Mr. Granoff holds numerous other titles within the peace and security movement. He has studied with the Sufi Master Bawa Muhaiyaddeen since his youth and is honored by receiving his namesake, Ahamed Muhaiyaddeen. He has lectured extensively all over the world on the subjects relating to peace, security, and human unity. For more information, visit the website of the Global Security Institute at www.gsinstitute.org.

Rev. Theodore M. Hesburgh, C.S.C., is president emeritus of the University of Notre Dame. Among his many academic and public service accomplishments, Father Hesburgh has served four Popes, three as permanent Vatican City representative to the International Atomic Energy Agency in Vienna from 1956 to 1970. Pope Paul VI also appointed him head of the Vatican representatives attending the 20th anniversary of the U.N.'s Human Rights Declaration in Teheran, Iran, in 1968, and six years later a member of the Holy See's United Nations delegation. He was a charter member of the U.S. Commission on Civil Rights, created in 1957, and he chaired the commission from 1969 to 1972. The author of several monographs, Father Hesburgh has also published two other books: *The Humane Imperative: A Challenge for the Year 2000*, published in 1974 by the Yale University press, and *The Hesburgh Papers: Higher Values in Higher Education*, published in 1979 by Andrews, McMeel, Inc.

Daisaku Ikeda is president of the Soka Gakkai International, a lay Buddhist organization pursuing the values of peace, culture and education and committed to fostering within individuals a sense of responsibility for the shared global community. He is also the founder of numerous cultural, educational and re-search institutions around the world. Prolific writer, poet and peace activist, he is recognized as one of the leading interpret-ers of Buddhism, bringing its timeless wisdom to bear on the many contemporary issues confronting humanity. Among the dozens of books he has written is the award-winning *For the Sake of Peace*. He received the United Nations Peace Award in 1983. Dr. Ikeda has been awarded many honorary doctorate degrees. For more information, visit Soka Gakkai International at www.sgi.org.

Craig Kielburger is the founder of Free the Children, which has become the largest international network of children help-ing children, having impacted over one million children in 35 countries. The organization has built more than 400 primary schools, providing daily education to over 35,000 children and has twice been nominated for the Nobel Peace Prize. Craig's work has been profiled on *60 Minutes*, CNN, CBC, *Oprah* and in the *New York Times*, *Time*, *The Economist* and *People Magazine*. Craig has traveled to more than 40 countries, speaking out in defense of children's rights. His first book, *Free the Children*, has been translated into eight languages and was the winner of the Christopher Book Award. For more information, visit www.freethechildren.org.

Marc Kielburger, J.D., is a Harvard graduate, Rhodes Scholar and Oxford-educated lawyer. He co-founded Leaders Today in 1999, which annually provides leadership training to more than 100,000 young people and has worked with the United Nations, State of the World Forum and numerous school boards throughout North America. His work has been profiled on CBC, CNN, BBC and in *Maclean's Report on Business* magazine and the *Los Angeles Times*. Marc has co-authored with his brother Craig Kielburger *Take Action!*, *Take More Action!* and *Me to We: Turning Self-Help on its Head*. Marc was recently chosen as one of Canada's "Top 40 leaders under the age of 40." For more information, visit www.leaderstoday.com.

David Krieger, J.D., Ph.D., is a founder of the Nuclear Age Peace Foundation, and has served as president of the Foundation since 1982. Under his leadership the Foundation has initiated many innovative and important projects for building peace, strengthening international law and abolishing nuclear weapons. Dr. Krieger has lectured throughout the United States, Europe and Asia on issues of peace, security, international law, and the abolition of nuclear weapons. Dr. Krieger is the author of many studies of peace in the Nuclear Age. Among the books he has most recently written or edited are *Albert Einstein: Peace Now*; *Today Is Not a Good Day for* War; *Peace 100 Ideas*; *Hope in a Dark Time*; *Reflections on Humanity's Future*; *The Poetry of Peace*; *Choose Hope*; *Nuclear Weapons and the World Court*; and *A Maginot Line in the Sky: International Perspectives on Ballistic Missile Defense*. For more information, visit the website of the Nuclear Age Peace Foundation at www.wagingpeace.org.

Mairead Corrigan Maguire founded the Community of the Peace People in 1976 along with Betty Williams and Ciaran McKeown. Mairead was the aunt of the three Maguire children who were hit by a getaway car after its driver was shot by a soldier. The deaths prompted a series of marches throughout Northern Ireland and abroad, all demanding an end to the violence. Mairead and Betty Williams went on to win the Nobel Peace Prize in 1976. Mairead is the recipient of numerous honors and awards, including the Norwegian People's Prize, and honorary doctorates from Yale University, the University of South Korea and the College of New Rochelle (New York). She has received special awards from Trinity College (Washington, D.C.) and St. Michael's College (Vermont). She was a special honoree of the United Nations "Women of Achievement" program in 1978 and of the American Academy of Achievement. In October 1990, she was named by Bishop Gerald O'Keefe to receive the 1990 "Pacem in Terris" Peace and Freedom Award in Davenport, Iowa. In June 1992, she received the Nuclear Age Peace Foundation's "Distinguished Peace Leadership Award." For more information, visit The Peace People online at www.peacepeople.com.

Rodrigo Carazo Odio is the former president of Costa Rica (1978-1982). He has been a statesman, educator, politician and farmer and is a respected activist in global peace initiatives and human rights concerns. His devotion to the promotion of friendship and peace in the world has won him international acclaim from many institutions in the world, and he has received many honorary degrees from prestigious universities. In 1978 he proposed the establishment of the University for Peace (UPEACE), on the basis that "if you want peace, prepare for peace." Chartered by the United Nations General Assembly on December 5, 1980, UPEACE is now a living reality in Ciudad Colón, Costa Rica. From 1983 to 1987, he was the first Rector at UPEACE and its Council President until 1988. For more information, visit University for Peace online at www. upeace.org.

Carah Ong is the Nuclear Age Peace Foundation's Advocacy and Research Director and is Director of the Foundation's Washington, DC office. She manages the Foundation's Turn the Tide Campaign to chart a new course for US nuclear policy. She also oversees the Foundation's Nuclear Files.org project, which provides educators, students and concerned citizens everywhere access to primary source documents, background information, and analysis on the political, legal and ethical challenges of the Nuclear Age. She serves on the Policy Education Board of the Alliance for Nuclear Accountability and on the organizing committee for the National Days of Action and Remembrance marking the 60th Anniversary of the US atomic bombings of Hiroshima and Nagasaki. Ong has published numerous articles and briefings on nuclear weapons and energy, and missile defense issues. She is co-editor of the book *A Maginot Line in the Sky: International Perspectives on Ballistic Missile Defense*. For more information, visit www.chartinganewcourse. org and www.nuclearfiles.org.

Dennis Rivers is a writer, teacher and activist who lives in Santa Barbara, California. He received his MA in interpersonal communication and human development from the Vermont College Graduate Program, after studying religious studies at UC Santa Barbara, and theology at the Graduate Theological Union in Berkeley. His books include *The Geometry of Dialogue*, *The Seven Challenges Workbook*, *Prayer Evolving*, and, most recently, *Turning Toward Life*. An earlier version of his essay on Hiroshima appeared as the preface to

Toby Lurie's book-length poem, *Hiroshima, A Symphonic Elegy for Spoken Voices*. For more information, visit www.nonukes.org.

Honorable Douglas Roche is a former Canadian Senator, Chairman of the Middle Powers Initiative, and an Officer of the Order of Canada. Roche was Canada's Ambassador for Disarmament from 1984 to 1989. He was elected Chairman of the United Nations Disarmament Committee in 1988. He has been awarded six honorary doctorates. He was a Canadian Member of Parliament from 1972 to 1984, specializing in the subjects of development and disarmament, and was the founding President of Parliamentarians for Global Action. He has received the Mahatma Gandhi Foundation for World Peace Award (1993, 1997), the Papal Medal for his service as Special Adviser on disarmament and security (1995), the United Nations Association's Medal of Honour (1995), the Pomerance Award (2000), the Gandhi, King, Ikeda Award (2003) and the Peace Award of the Canadian Islamic Congress (2003). Senator Roche is the author of seventeen books, including *The Human Right to Peace* (Novalis, 2003). For more information, visit Senator Roche's official website at www.douglasroche.ca.

Dame Anita Roddick is founder of The Body Shop and an eminent author, speaker and human rights activist. Dame Roddick is a graduate of Newton Park College of Higher Education, Bath. In 1997, Dame Roddick helped launch The New Academy of Business, a Master's degree course at Bath University with the aim of reforming business education for the new century. Dame Roddick is the author of five books: *Body & Soul* (Ebury Press, 1991); *Business as Unusual* (Thorsons, 2000); *Take it Personally* (Thorsons, 2001); *Brave Hearts, Rebel Spirits* (Anita Roddick Books, 2003); and, *A Revolution in Kindness* (Anita Roddick Books, 2003). Dame Roddick has received numerous awards for her work, including most recently being named Dame Commander of the British Empire. She serves as trustee to a number of international organizations, including the Nuclear Age Peace Foundation. For more information, visit Dame Anita Roddick's official website at www.anitaroddick.com.

Masami Saionji is a spiritual leader and the Chairperson of the Goi Peace Foundation and the World Peace Prayer Society. Descended from the Royal Ryukyu Family of Okinawa, she succeeds the work of her adoptive father, Masahisa Goi, who advocated the universal prayer "May Peace Prevail on Earth" in Japan after the Second World War. She is a respected lecturer at international conferences, and has also traveled around the world leading World Peace Prayer Ceremonies in many countries and at the Untied Nations and other international organizations. She is the author of many books including *The Golden Key to Happiness*, *Infinite Happiness*, and *You Are the Universe*, all of which have been published in several languages. For more information, visit the Goi Peace Foundation online at www.goipeace.or.jp.

Howard Zinn is a professor, historian, activist, World War II veteran, and best-selling author. He is perhaps best-known for his popular history book of the United States from the perspective of the working class and "minority" groups, *A People's History of the United States*. For years, Zinn has combined academics with activism. In the 50s, 60s and 70s he studied and participated in the civil rights and antiwar movements. Zinn established himself as a radical critic that spared neither the liberal establishment nor the conservative powers-that-be. Since 1964, he has taught government at Boston University. He has written numerous articles and books including *The Zinn*

Reader, You Can't Be Neutral on a Moving Train, and the play *Emma.* Zinn received the Lannan Foundation Literary Award for Nonfiction and the Eugene V. Debs award for his writing and political activism. For more information, visit Howard Zinn's official website at www.howardzinn.org.

NUCLEAR AGE PEACE FOUNDATION

The Nuclear Age Peace Foundation is a non-profit, non-partisan international organization on the Roster in consultative status to the United Nations Economic and Social Council. Founded in 1982, the Foundation is a catalyst in enhancing global security by initiating and supporting efforts to reduce nuclear dangers; strengthening international law and institutions; and working to inspire and empower a new generation of peace leaders.

Vision: Our vision is a world at peace, free of the threat of war and free of weapons of mass destruction.

Mission: To advance initiatives to eliminate the nuclear weapons threat to all life, to foster the global rule of law, and to build an enduring legacy of peace through education and advocacy.

Programs

Enhancing Security by Reducing Nuclear Dangers

Since its inception, the cornerstone of the Foundation's work has been to enhance security by working to reduce and eliminate nuclear threats. The Foundation has provided leadership in the establishment of coalitions, including the Middle Powers Initiative, a coalition of eight international organizations working with governments and civil society toward a treaty banning nuclear weapons; and Abolition 2000, a Global Network for the Elimination of Nuclear Weapons. We helped found and continue to provide leadership to the International Network of Engineers and Scientists for Global Responsibility (INES). In 1998, we also developed and launched an Appeal to Eliminate the Nuclear Weapons Threat to Humanity. More than 100 world leaders, including 38 Nobel Laureates, have signed and endorsed the Appeal.

Strengthening International Law

Respect for the rule of law is fundamental to the success of democratic systems throughout the world. Treaties among nations can only exist in a world that respects international law and provides sufficient authority to international bodies to monitor and enforce those agreements. The Foundation participates each year in conferences at the United Nations seeking progress on nuclear non-proliferation and disarmament. In 2002, the Foundation established an annual symposium on critical issues of international law. Topics have included establishing an effective international criminal court; developing a United Nations Emergency Peace Service capable of responding to acts of genocide and gross human rights violations; and charting a new course for US nuclear policy within a multilateral framework.

Educating and Empowering Youth

The Foundation's Youth Outreach Initiative is on the cutting edge of programs to inspire and empower a new generation of peace leaders. It is one of the few nationally sustained peace programs involving high school and college students. The Initiative includes Peace Leadership Trainings, educational curricula, the Swackhamer Peace Essay Contest, internships, forums and public advocacy campaigns. Thousands of students have participated in these activities and many have gone on to become leaders on their campuses, in their communities and in organizations around the world.

Providing Quality Independent Research and Information

An informed citizenry is necessary to elect responsible decision-makers. In turn, informed decision-makers are necessary to create effective changes in policy. The Foundation is a leader in public education and provides independent analysis to decision-makers around the world. Our public education is conducted primarily through our websites, which attract more than two million visitors each year. Other means to disseminate information include *The Sunflower*, a free e-newsletter sent to some 10,000 subscribers worldwide; reports and briefing books; books, and lectures.

The power of one voice can become an unconquerable force when joined with millions of others seeking the same goal. We invite you to add your voice for a more secure world. For more information, please visit us online at:

www.wagingpeace.org

Nuclear Age Peace Foundation
Headquarters
PMB 121, 1187 Coast Village Road, Suite 1
Santa Barbara, CA 93108-2794
(805) 965-3443
Washington DC Office
322 Fourth Street NE
Washington, DC 20002
(202) 543-4100, ext. 105